AN ILLUSTRATED GUIDE TO

MODERN
BOMBERS

Bill Gunston

AN ILLUSTRATED GUIDE TO
MODERN
BOMBERS

Bill Gunston

PRENTICE HALL PRESS
New York London Toronto Sydney Tokyo

Prentice Hall Press
Gulf + Western Building
One Gulf + Western Plaza
New York, New York 10023

An Arco Military Book

Published by the Prentice Hall Trade Division

PRENTICE HALL PRESS and colophon are registered
trademarks of Simon & Schuster Inc.

Originally published in 1988 in the United Kingdom by
Salamander Books Ltd., 52 Bedford Row, London WC1R 4LR.

This book may not be sold outside the United States
of America and Canada.

Library of Congress Cataloging-in-Publication Data

Gunston, Bill
　An illustrated guide to modern bombers.
　(An Arco military book)
　1. Bombers. 2. Bombers — Pictorial works. I. Title.
II. Title: Modern bombers. III. Series.
UG1242.B6G89　1988　　　358.4'2　　　87-47992
ISBN 0-13-453268-6

10 9 8 7 6 5 4 3 2 1

First Prentice Hall Press Edition

Credits

Author: Bill Gunston is an internationally respected author of many books
on military aviation. He is a frequent broadcaster, contributor to several
defense periodicals, and is Assistant Compiler of *Jane's All The World's
Aircraft*.

Editor: Ray Bonds
Designed by: Geoff Denney Associates
Diagrams: TIGA
Filmset by The Old Mill
Color reproduction by Kentscan Ltd.
Printed in Belgium by Proost International Book Production, Turnhout.

Photographs: The publishers wish to thank all the official governmental
archives, aircraft and system manufacturers, and private individuals, who
have supplied photographs for this book.

Contents

Introduction

Everyone knows that bombers are usually large and awesome aircraft which fly over enemy territory and drop bombs. Yet this popular scenario has had a very short life indeed, despite being extremely important in the two world wars. Although in April 1982 a traditional bomber — the Vulcan — made a traditional bombing raid on the runway at Port Stanley, in the Falkland Islands, this ought not to blind us to the fact that, since 20 years previously, such a mission was an aberration, a throwback to a former age. Today, any attempt at such a mission would make the defenders say, incredulously, 'Hey, let me take a good look at this guy before I clobber him!'

In fact, the history of the bomber is a microcosm of the story of technology, allied with that of warfare in general. It begins with a few pioneers and visionaries trying to accomplish something that has never been done before. Gradually their efforts attract the attention of governments, pursestrings are loosened and it all begins to happen. Often as the result of particular events or campaigns, experts jump to wrong conclusions. By the start of World War II the bomber was widely regarded as the weapon that would win the war. At the end of World War II, however, the bomber was the subject of vociferous argument. Some said the bomber had won — or at least materially shortened — the war, while others claimed it had proved totally ineffective. Since August 1945 the arguments over the strategic value of bombers have never ceased to rage. The picture is confused by the growing capability of thousands of attack aircraft, which look like fighters and so are universally called fighters by the media. A further factor of overwhelming importance is the emergence in the 1950s of the intercontinental ballistic missile (ICBM). Together with the submarine-launched ballistic missile (SLBM) the ICBM gives any major power the ability, unfailingly and without opposition, the wipe out

cities, ports and other major centres in enemy heartlands, without hazarding any of its own personnel and without giving its enemy more than a few minutes of warning. Inevitably, this has relegated the bomber slightly into a secondary place. But before going further, we ought to cover the ground in a little more detail.

The bombers of 1945 looked utterly different from those of 1914, and were vastly more capable; but both generations of aeroplane were trying to do the same job in the same way, and the differences were merely of degree.

Genesis

The first 'bomber' was an Etrich Taube monoplane of the Italian Air Flotilla engaged in fighting the Turks near Tripoli. Flown by Second Lieutenant Giulio Gavotti, it dropped Cipelli explosive grenades on enemy troops at Ain Zara and the Taguira Oasis on 1 November 1911. In 1912 various aircraft dropped bombs during the Balkan wars. But to call these aircraft bombers would be euphemistic. They were hardly modified at all, and the bombs were usually carried loose in the cockpit and dropped over the side by hand. At least one pilot had bombs suspended by loops of string from his feet, and when over the target he kicked them off!

Gradually arrangements were made for properly designed bomb racks, coupled in some cases with crude aiming mechanisms to direct the bombs towards their target. The first raid by what could truly be called a bomber took place on 8 October

Above right: Some of the earliest bombing missions were flown by the Russian Czar's 'Squadron of Flying Ships' with various kinds of Sikorsky IM bomber.

Right: In World War I Britain's Royal Navy ordered Mr Handley Page to build the 0/400 (later operated by the RFC and RAF).

1914. Two Sopwith Tabloids — tiny 80hp biplanes — of Britain's Royal Naval Air Service (RNAS) each dropped two 20lb Hales bombs from underwing racks on the railway station and Zeppelin sheds at Cologne, destroying a new airship. By this time, the commander of the RNAS had asked designer Frederick Handley Page to build a giant bomber, 'a bloody paralyser of an aeroplane', and Handley Page bombers were to play a major part in World War I. But the pioneer heavy bombers came from other countries. Russia had its EVK, the Squadron of Flying Ships, equipped with huge four-engined IM-type bombers designed by Igor Sikorsky (much later the American pioneer of the helicopter). Italy had proud regiments of Caproni bombers, which flew tough 10-hour missions in freezing conditions across the Alps.

After World War I, several influential officers claimed the bomber would be the key weapon in any future war. In the USA, the flamboyant General Billy Mitchell bombed and sank huge warships during experiments designed to prove that bombers were more important than navies, and he deliberately courted a court-martial becuase of his outspoken campaigning. In Britain, Air Marshal Sir Hugh Trenchard, 'father of the RAF', likewise adhered to the view that the bomber was the supreme weapon. This belief appeared to be confirmed by the various rather falsely contrived air exercise mounted by all major air forces during peace time. The horrifying bombing of cities in Spain and China in 1936-39 did nothing to lessen the belief that the bomber would sweep all before it.

World War II

During World War II, Britain and the USA spent huge sums building up powerful forces of large four-engined bombers. Germany and the Soviet Union, meanwhile, concentrated on smaller twin-engined aircraft that were intended to fly missions closely linked with land battles, helping to clear a path for their huge armies. Only Japan followed the Western democracies in trying to build up long-range strategic airpower, but tried to do it with twin-engined aircraft which, lacking armour and other protection, tended to catch fire when shot at. Only Britain and the USA put real effort behind the strategic bomber, and they built up the greatest bomber forces the world had ever seen. The RAF concentrated on night bombing, gradually devloping amazing skills in the new art of electronics in order to find targets and confuse the enemy. The US Army Air Force (USMF) sent out its huge bomber forces over Europe by day, partly to hit targets and parly to bring the enemy air forces to battle. Over Japan, the new Boeing B-29 Superfortress, flying faster and higher than any previous bomber, switched from day to night operations.

By the summer of 1945, Germany and Japan had been absolutely devastated. Most impartial observers maintain that the bombing campaigns did have an important effect on the ability of those countries to wage war, but in fact neither civilian morale nor industrial production were greatly affected. Whether the Allied effort might have been better applied elsewhere will remain a matter for debate. What is beyond dispute, however, is that at the end of World War II a totally new situation had arisen. The development of jet bombers meant that attacking aircraft could now fly twice as high and twice as fast as previously. And the development of nuclear bombs meant that a single bomber could now destroy a city, a task that previously had required a thousand or more aircraft. Quite suddenly, the bomber had become unimaginably more deadly.

Right: Boeing's B-29 set totally new standards in the technology of the strategic bomber.

Below: Britain's Avro Lancaster was an outstanding medium-altitude trucking system.

The USAF's Strategic Air Command (SAC) built up enormous global strength with giant piston-engined and jet bombers, backed up by the new capability of refuelling in flight to reach anywhere on Earth. Its 'deterrence' was reflected in its motto 'Peace is our Profession'; by wielding a so-called big stick it could, so the argument ran, prevent any rash act from escalating into a major war (but it still proved unable to prevent local wars all over the world). In parallel, the ICBM and SLBM were developed, each able to carry one or more nuclear warheads accurately to targets on the other side of the globe. These competed with bombers for funds, and tended increasingly to restrict the latter to conventional warfare and to attacks on moving targets such as armies and navies. Fixed targets, such as cities, airfields and ICBM silos, can be attacked far more effectively by missiles.

During the 1950s the USA, Britain, Soviet Union and to a limited degree France, all built up strategic bomber forces. As early as 1950, far-sighted designers had planned bombers and winged cruise missiles that could fly long distances at very low level, making it much more difficult for their presence to be detected by defending radar networks. Curiously, the obvious need for such aircraft was ignored, and instead the cry was to fly ever faster and higher. The USAF even put a supersonic bomber into service, even though this aircraft, the Convair B-58, had too short a range to fly most of SAC's missions. The reasoning behind the actions seemed obscure.

Britain's V-Force

In Britain Vickers-Armstrongs flew the prototype Valiant four-jet bomber in 1951, this aircraft being designed to operate at heights of 36,000ft (10,500m) and above. In 1953 Vickers flew the prototype Valiant Mk 2, specially strengthened the operate at low levels and with maximum speed at sea level increased from 414 to 552mph (660k/h-888k/h). The MK 2 was ignored, and RAF Bomber Command received 104 Valiants of the Mk 1 type. In 1962 it was belatedly realized that in order to penetrate defended airspace bombers had to fly at low level, and the Valiants were duly painted in low-level camouflage and operated at heights around 500ft (152m). Within 18 months their structures were suffering from dangerous fatigue cracking, because their version, unlike the purpose-built MK 2, had not been designed to fly at full throttle in the dense turbulent air near the ground. In October 1964 the Valiants were grounded.

Precision guided

The Valiant was one of the few big jet bombers to go into action, four squadrons carrying out missions against Egypt with free-fall bombs in the autumn of 1956. Though later marks of this aircraft had additional capability in the strategic reconnaissance role, and as air-refuelling tankers, the Valiant was never equipped with any weapons other than free-fall bombs. Soon after World War II, the Ministry of Supply had ordered the development of two sizes of bomb fitted with precision guidance via a radio link from the bomber associated with a TV camera in the weapon's nose. But this impressive programme, code named Blue Boar, was cancelled in 1954 just as it was ready to enter production.

Above: The Avro Vulcan was a bold answer to a challenging demand. This B.2 is seen in the 1960s, in low-level camouflage before being fitted with ECM gear and terrain-following radar.

Below: Seen here serving with the USAF's 43rd Bomb Wing, the B-50D was a much more powerful development of the B-29; they were soon converted into crew trainers and tankers.

The Valiant itself was regarded as only an interim type. Strangely, Britain built four types of four-jet bomber, all to do essentially the same job. Three of these went into service in numbers. The two later aircraft were the Avro Vulcan and Handley Page Victor, both excellent aircraft and both destined for a long active life. The Vulcan and Victor were each intended to carry a supersonic rocket-propelled cruise missile, known in Britain as a 'stand-off bomb', to enable large thermonuclear (H-bomb) warheads to be delivered on to the most heavily defended targets — through airspace which the bombers themselves might not be able to penetrate. This missile, called Blue Steel, was as big as a fighter, weighed 15,000lb (6804kg), and could fly up to 200 miles (322km) after being released from under the belly of the bomber. Blue Steel got into service, in June 1962, and small numbers were deployed in squadrons equipped with both the Vulcan B.2 and Victor B.2. These Mk 2 aircraft had both been developed to fly at higher altitudes in the mistaken belief that this would help them to avoid being shot down. After 1962, however,

both had to come down to low level in order to try and escape detection by hostile radars. They also ran into political problems.

'Flexible response'

One of the political problems was that the 1950s policy of 'massive retaliation' using nuclear weapons at the first sign of any enemy attack was replaced by one of so-called 'controlled' or 'flexible' response, using ordinary high-explosive bombs. Each of the 'V-bombers' (Valiant, Vulcan and Victor) had been designed to carry early nuclear bombs which were so large that their weapon bays were capable of accommodating considerable loads of conventional bombs. The first two could carry 21 bombs of 1,000lb (454kg) size, and the Victor 35. In 1960, plans were drawn up to equip the Vulcan, and possibly the Victor, to launch Skybolt ALBMs (air-launched ballistic missiles). The latter were large

Below: Early Convair B-36B-5 bombers of the US 8th AF at Carswell AFB. In some respects these were the biggest bombers ever put into service.

Top: Britain's Canberra proved so versatile it was developed for 17 different roles. This one was converted as a T.11 to train radar operators of Javelins (escort).

Above: Another version of the Canberra was the US-built Martin B-57B, a tactical intruder which, as seen here, operated intensively in the Vietnam War.

American missiles weighing 11,300lb (5126kg) and possessing a range after release from the bomber of 1,150 miles (1850km). These plans collapsed, however, and the British government decided instead to adopt a totally different kind of nuclear deterrent based on SLBMs, of the American Polaris type. From that time on, RAF bombers played a secondary role assigned to Supreme Allied Commander Europe (SACEUR) in the low-level role, carrying conventional bombs only. The Blue Steel cruise missiles were withdrawn.

Bombers into tankers

The sudden grounding of the Valiants in 1964 left the RAF with no tankers, and to fill the gap a crash programme was undertaken to convert the Victor B.1 bombers into tankers. Later, in the 1970s, the Victor B.2 bombers were likewise converted into tankers, the task in this cased amounting to an almost complete rebuild. A handful of Mk 2 Victors and Vulcans were also converted into strategic reconnaissance aircraft, with the weapon bays occuped by large pallets carrying batteries of cameras and, later, infra-red and electronic reconnaissance systems. Gradually the whole V-force was withdrawn until, in April 1982, just a handful of Vulcan bombers and Victor tankers remained. Then all hell broke loose with the Argentinian invasion of the Falklands, and in a matter of days refuelling probes were found and attached, bomb bays were once more equipped for conventional bombs and AGM-45 Shrike anti-radar missiles were obtained from the USA and attached under Vulcan wings. By means of successive in-flight refuelling, 'Black Buck' missions were flown to bomb the Port Stanley runway from Ascension Island, a round trip of 8,000 miles that was accomplished in 15h 45min, by far the longest bombing missions in history.

The American challenge

The Strategic Air Command of the USAF, formed in March 1946, started off with two giant advantages over all adversaries: the B-29 and the atom bomb. The B-29 flew higher and faster than any other bomber, it had remotely controlled defensive gun turrets and was at least a generation ahead of the previous 'heavies' that had fought throughout World War II. As for the atom bomb, this awesome weapon made a single bomber as deadly as a whole armada had been previously. Yet by 1952 the Soviet Union possessed both these advances, the one gained by direct copying of B-29s which had landed in what the aircrews thought was friendly territory, and the other by straightforward spying. From the Tupolev Tu-4, the B-29 copy, the Soviet designers were to derive a succession of more formidable bombers with turboprop and jet propulsion which, as described later, are still in service.'

From June 1950 the USAF B-29s were back at war, in Korea. In the final year of World War II, hundreds of VB-1 Azons had been dropped from B-17s and B-24s. 'VB' stood for vertical bomb, and the name Azon came from 'azimuth only', indicating that it could be steered by radio in direction only. Even this limited amount of guidance made the Azons very effective, and many difficult targets received direct hits. Development of many other VBs proceeded apace, and by 1950 some B-29 units were equipped with a monster called VB-13 Tarzon. This comprised a 12,000lb (5443kg) bomb with a flare at the back, aft of an octagonal tail fitted with radio-directed controls to guide it onto its target. Tarzons demolished many crucial targets in Korea, including rail bridges, road bridges and a large dam.

The amazing B-47

On the day the Korean war started, Boeing had flown the first production example of the B-47 Stratojet. Few aircraft have ever been so boldly designed, nor looked so futuristic in comparison with those around it. At a time when other bombers had traditional airframes, crews of around a

dozen, piston engines and an array of defensive gun turrets, the B-47 had wings and tail swept back at 35°, six jet engines in underwing pods, a crew of three and no turrets except a remotely controlled barbette in the tail. At a stroke, it more than doubled the speed and added about 10,000ft (300m) to the attack height of bombers, though it needed inflight refuelling to fly strategic missions. Well over 2,000 of these beautiful aircraft were to be built, but their only combat duty was to be in the hazardous role of electronic reconnaissance, before and during the Vietnam war.

When the B-47 was designed it was thought that the planned long-range heavy bomber, the B-52 Stratofortress, would have to be powered by turboprops in order to achieve the desired range. In 1960-51 it became apparent that by using no fewer than eight of a new, powerful and very fuel-efficient turbojet, the J57, it would be possible to make the B-52 a jet; Boeing flew the prototype in April 1952. At the time it was the

Above: A mighty challenge to its designers and crews, the B-58A was at the same time a great aircraft. It carried fuel and bomb(s) in a droppable pod.

Below: Almost the only bomber faster than the B-58 (one here acting as escort), the six-engined XB-70 Valkyrie never went into service.

heaviest and most expensive bomber in history, but it was what SAC needed and, under extreme pressure, it was readied for production. The B-52 entered service in 1955, but, unlike the B-47, its manufacture was broken down into eight different variants, each introducing new features.

Altogether 744 were delivered, the most numerous model being the B-520 of which 193 were built. What nobody expected was that, for various reasons, no successor would enter service for more than 30 years, and that the B-52G and H would soldier on into the 1990s.

17

No bomber has ever been subjected to such prolonged and complex modification and updating, over so long a period, as the B-52. Like other bombers in the 1960s, the massive B-52 was forced to come down from the stratosphere and fly at low level in order to penetrate hostile airspace. It suffered more structural problems than most in adapting to this harsh new environment, and at the same time had to be fitted with a seemingly endless succession of new weapons, defensive counter-measures, offensive avionics and other new devices, altogether amounting to several times more than the aircraft themselves had cost when new. In the Vietnam war, large numbers of various versions were modified to carry unprecedented loads of conventional bombs, coth internally and externally, and they put down a greater tonnage of bombs than in any previous conflict. They also took on large numbers of (SAMs), though the latter were of such an early type that the score-sheet, which favoured the B-52s, could lead to dangerously false conclusions. Today the B-52G and H remain in full service, armed with conventional and nuclear bombs, SRAMs (Short-Range Attack Missiles), ALCM (Air-Launched Cruise Missiles) and, in the anti-ship role, GBU-15(V) precision conventional weapons and Harpoon sea-skimming cruise missiles.

A Mach 2 bomber

The thunderous B-58 Hustler was the world's first bomber able to fly at Mach 2, but it was costly to operate and had a relatively short active life. The amazing XB-70 Valkyrie was probably the most powerful combat aircraft ever built, but it never went into service. Instead, after 10-years of study, the swing-wing B-1A was flown in 1974, only to be cancelled in 1977. Rockwell and the USAF continued to work on the B-1 and in 1981 President Reagan gave the go-ahead to a force of 100 B-1Bs which are now mostly in service. Compared with the B-1A the B model may look the same, but it has several subtle differences. Instead of flying at Mach 2 in the stratosphere it flies at 500mph at tree-top height. Instead of having an ejectable crew capsule it has conventional ejection seats, and instead of complex variable engine inlets it has plain fixed ones. But its ability to penetrate defended airspace without being detected has been many times multiplied, partly though so-called 'stealth' characteristics and partly because it carries the biggest load of defensive electronics — detectors, anaylsers, jammers and other countermeasures — ever packed into a single aircraft.

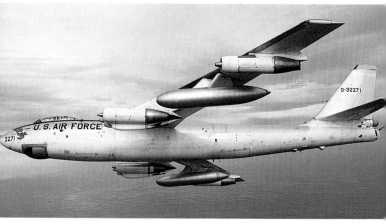

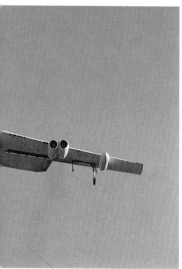

Top: A Boeing ERB-47H, one of the variants of the Stratojet converted for Clandestine (and often perilous) electronic reconnaissance missions which involved overflying unfriendly territory.

Above: The B-47E formed the backbone of the USAF's Strategic Air Command in the 1950s (the last was withdrawn in 1966). In all 2,042 B-47s were built, a remarkable total for a 100-ton combat aircraft in peacetime.

Left: Taken on 1 February 1956, this photograph shows one of the first B-52s of the USAF 93rd Heavy Bombardment Wing taking off from Castle AFB.

The Soviet response

Like the B-52s, the chief bombers of the Soviet Union have had an incredibly long active life. Around 1950, with the Tu-4 in full production, the Tupolev bureau had developed impressive enlarged versions, the Tu-80 and Tu-85. But these two aircraft were not deployed in numbers. Instead, the VVS (Soviet air force) waited for swept-wing aircraft powered by gas turbines. First to fly, in 1952, was the Tu-16 (service designation). Called the 'Badger' by NATO, this was a clean six-seater in the class of the Valiant but powered by just two enormous turbojets buried in the wing roots. Like the Boeing B-47, over 2,000 were built, but the Soviet aircraft has appeared in far more versions than the American aircraft, performing innumerable and more diverse tasks over a much longer period. Virtually all of these variants are still in service. Even more remarkable is the monster Tu-95, designated Tu-20 by the VVS and called 'Bear' by NATO. When this aircraft appeared in 1954 few Western observers could understand how it could have swept wings and tail as well as propellers. Little was it suspected that this global-ranging machine would remain in production in new versions into the late 1980s!

Soviet supersonics

With the Tu-105 (VVS Tu-22, NATO ('Blinder'), a Soviet equivalent of the B-58 was created, though with just two engines mounted at the tail. It is relatively limited in range, but was used as the basis for a much longer-ranged aircraft with swinging outer wings. This in turn was the basis for the Tu-26/22M (NATO 'Backfire') which is now serving in large numbers with both the strategic regiments and also with the AV-MF (Soviet naval air force), mainly on oceanic missions. There has been much argument about the degree to which these aircraft threaten the USA directly. With the benefit of in-flight refuelling, they clearly have the ability to fly from Soviet territory to targets in the USA. Yet with such vast forces of ICBMs and SLBMs at their disposal, the Soviet planners do not need manned bombers for such missions, unless of course the target

Right: Pilot and copilot of a B-52H, the final and longest-ranged version of this famous bomber, en route to Darwin, Australia, for an exercise in 1982. At that date the EVS (p.104) had been installed.

Below: Visibly distinguished by its TF33 turbofan engines, the B-52H also introduced a new ASG-21 rear defence system with a 20mm 'Gatling gun'. Long since upgraded to fire SRAMs, these aircraft are now being modified to launch the AGM-86B.

happens to be a moving one. Nevertheless, the Tupolev bureau has now developed a much bigger bomber, first seen in 1981 and dubbed 'Blackjack' by NATO. This strongly resembles the USAF's B-1B, but is appreciably larger. American 'guesstimates' credit both these Soviet swing-wing giants as having the ability to fly at Mach 2 at high altitude, despite the fact that such behaviour would today be suicidal in defended airspace. Like all bombers, the Backfire and Blackjack make no sense whatever unless they are used at subsonic speed at the lowest possible height, and deployed only against moving targets which cannot be hit by intercontinental missiles, such as fleets of warships.

China and France

China has built large numbers of two long-established kinds of bomber of Soviet design, the Il-28 (called the H-5 in China) and the Tu-16 (called the H-6). The latter has been developed in indigenous Chinese versions, with locally produced radar and cruise missiles. In due course updated Chinese bombers may be expected to appear. The only other country to use true bombers is France, which in 1963-67 built 62 Dassault Mirage IVA bombers each looking very like a Mirage III fighter but considerably larger and twin-engined. By adopting a unique system of 'buddy' inflight refuelling using aircraft in pairs, these Mach 2 aircraft have demonstrated their ability to fly quite long missions using free-fall bombs. Eighteen of these aircraft have now been completely upgraded to Mirage IVP standard and fitted with ASMP supersonic cruise missiles to increase their effectiveness against heavily defended targets.

Low level, lower risk

Like most of the world's bombers, the Mirage IVs were designed to fly fast and high, but in order to survive have been forced to come down to very low levels. Flying in dense turbulent air near the Earth's surface enables bombers to penetrate defended airspace with a reduced probability of being detected by defending radars. It has other less desirable effects, however. It greatly increases the rate of fuel consumption, so the effective radius of action is drastically reduced. It subjects the airframe to violent buffeting, and can not only induce fatigue but can give the crew such a rough ride that their efficiency falls right away until they can no longer perform the task they were assigned. To attack at low level calls for a specially designed aircraft that has a very strong structure and a small, highly-loaded wing with the shortest possible span. It also requires a special TFR (terrain-following radar) which can navigate the aircraft along the contours of the land, enabling it to fly safely over or around obstructions — during day, night or through bad weather.

Above: A close-up of the tail of a Tu-95 'Bear-D', showing gunner (with twin 23mm cannon) and an observer in side blister.

Right: This 'Badger-D' electronic reconnaissance aircraft is one of many current versions modified from Tu-16 bombers.

The first aircraft able to do this was the USAF's F-111, originally planned as a fighter. One version of this aircraft, the FB-111A, has served successfully with USAF Strategic Air Command as a bomber, and is currently being upgraded for further service. A much newer aircraft in this class is the European Tornado, though this is not included in this book because it is classed as a tactical attack aircraft and would not normally be required to fly strategic missions.

The advent of 'stealth'

In Vietnam, early versions of the F-111 repeatedly demonstrated that their thrilling capability of attacking at full throttle just above the Earth'sz surface, even at night or in cloud, protected them from ever being 'painted' by enemy radar. But an F-111 can still be seen by radars sited on mountain peaks or carried aloft in interceptor aircraft, and for some 10 years it has been appreciated that Sir Robert Watson Watt, the 'father of radar', was absolutely correct when he said in 1936 that the designers of future bombers would try to make their aircraft as 'invisible' to radar as possible. About 40 years later this prediction, designers finally realised that what is today called 'stealth' design is vital to all future bombers. In essence, a stealth aircraft aims to fly through the airspace of its enemy unnoticed. This is the most difficult task aircraft designers have ever attempted.

To design a true stealth aircraft is, of course, impossible; it makes no sense to try to hide a bomber from enemy radars if it can be seen clearly with the eyes, if it makes a thunderous noise and if its engines spout flame and hot gas which can be detected by infra-red sensors from 100 miles away! Aircraft may be seen against snow, ocean, grass, desert, cities, blue sky and white clouds, so making a bomber invisible is no easy task. Moreover, modern bombers invariably have large jet engines which pump out as much heat as 10,000 cars all revving up at once, so the problems of escaping detection from infra-red sensors are enormous. Yet the probability of detection can be minimised.

Radar cross-section

The easiest part of stealth design is to reduce the RCS (radar cross-section), making the aircraft less visible on enemy surveillance radars. This can be done by making the aircraft physically sm aller, by moulding its shape into smooth curves rather than large, flattish reflecting surfaces, by hiding the fronts of the highly reflective engines deep inside the inlet ducts, by adopting special constructional methods which at-

tempt to prevent any radar signal from being reflected back along its incident path, and by covering parts of the aircraft with RAM (radar-absorbent material) which effectively soaks up radar waves without reflecting them.

The first stealth, or 'low-observable', aircraft known to have entered service is a modest reconnaissance$strike aircraft (possibly called the RS-19) built for the USAF by Lockheed. It has not been included in this book becuase it could hardly be called a bomber, even though it is capable of flying tactical attack missions. It does, however, provide an important background of the service experience which has assisted the design of a totally new ATB (Advanced Technology Bomber) now in final assembly for the USAF by Northrop. When this enters service in the early 1990s it will once again give the USAF a capability possessed by no other air force, at least until the ever-alert Soviet designers produce their own versions, on which they must have been working for several years. But then again, to every weapon there has always been a counter-weapon. The problems of building the truly undetectable bomber are so obviously daunting that even the crew of the future ATB will feel the adrenalin flowing as they cross the hostile frontier. Let's hope it doesn't ever happen for real.

Above: During development of the French Mirage IVA one task was to prove the use of a battery of jettisonable rockets for thrusting the fully loaded aircraft off short strips.

Below: The seventh F-111A tests separation of 16 stores carried on all eight pylons, the theoretical maximum external load. In USAF service eight pylons have not been used.

Avro (Hawker Siddeley, British Aerospace) Vulcan

Vulcan B.1, B.2

Origin: A.V. Roe & Company Ltd, UK (later Hawker Siddeley Aviation, later British Aerospace, Manchester).

Type: Strategic bomber.

Engines: Four Bristol (later Bristol Siddeley, later Rolls-Royce) Olympus turbojets, (B.1) 11,000lb (4,990kg) thrust Olympus 101, later 13,500lb (6,124kg) Olympus 104, (B.2) 17,000lb (7,711kg) thrust Olympus 201, later 20,000lb (9,072kg) Olympus 301.

Dimensions: Span (B.1) 99ft (30.18m), (B.2) 111ft (33.83m); length (B.1) 97ft 1in (29.6m), (B.2, without probe) 99ft 11in (30.46m), (B.2 with probe) 105ft 6in (32.15m); height (B.1) 26ft 1in (7.94m), (B.2) 27ft 2in (8.26m); wing area (B.1) 3,554sq ft (330.17m²), (B.2) 3,964sq ft (368.27m²).

Weights: Empty weights never published; maximum loaded, about 170,000lb (77,112kg) for the B.1 and 250,000lb (113,400kg) for the B.2 family.

Performance: Maximum speed at high altitude (B.1) 620mph (998km/h), (B.2) 645mph (1,038km/h); cruising speed 490-600mph (789-966km/h); service ceiling (B.1) 52,000ft (15,850m), (B.2) 61,000ft (18,600m); range with maximum bombload (B.1) about 3,500 miles (5,633km), (B.2) 4,600 miles (7,400km).

Armament: Internal bomb bay for various nuclear bombs or up to 21 (three groups of seven) GP bombs of 1,000lb (454kg); B.2 only built with provision to launch one Blue Steel Mk 1 supersonic stand-off cruise missile carried semi-externally; no defensive armament.

History: First flight (prototype) 30 August 1952, (production B.1) 4 February 1955, (production B.2) 30 August 1958; final delivery 14 January 1965.

User: UK (RAF).

Deployment: Like its rival, the Victor, the Vulcan was designed to meet Specification B.35/46 calling for a bomber to carry a 10,000lb nuclear bomb for 3,350 nautical miles at 500 knots, with an over-target height of 50,000ft. For some reason it was stipulated that the loaded weight should not exceed 100,000lb, and this requirement proved extremely difficult to meet. The only way the Avro design team in Manchester could get around the problem was to create a dramatically new aircraft of tailless delta (triangular) shape, the wings then being so thick that lightweight skins could be used. The depth of the inner ▶

Above: Three B.2s (**XM605, XH561 and XJ784**) at dispersal, almost certainly at Akrotiri, Cyprus. In the background are Victor K.1A tankers and Phantom FGR.2s.

Below: A B.2 (with fin-cap electronic-warfare antennas) of No 44 Sqn, which in 1942 was first with Avro's Lancaster.

► wings enabled the four engines to be buried inside them, fed from inlets in the leading edge. This also provided ample volume for fuel, and for the Dowty main landing gears with eight small tyres on each leg, retracted forwards into the wing just outboard of the engine air ducts. The crew of five were accommodated in the double-deck pressurized compaprtment in the nose, the pilots side-by-side on ejection seats under a jettisonable fighter-shape canopy and the nav-radar, nav-plotter and AEO (air electronics officer) facing backwards to the rear. An enduring fault of the Vulcan was that in any emergency it was unlikely that three back-seat men would escape.

Avro produced 45 Vulcan B.1 and B.1A bombers between 1956 and March 1959. These were all powered by the Olympus 100 (101 to 104) series engine and had the original wing, initially with a straight leading edge and quickly modified with a drooped and kinked leading edge, giving better handling at high altitude. The Mk 1A had an enlarged tailcone filled with ECM equipment;

almost every Mk 1 in service (with RAF Nos 27, 44, 61, 83, 101 and 617 Squadrons) was brought up to Mk 1A standard. The Mk 2 was planned to offer greater over-target height, as well as greater range and other advantages. Its main difference was that the outer wing panels were greatly enlarged, reducing the thickness/chord ratio, and instead of having inboard elevators and outboard ailerons the entire trailing edge was occupied by eight powered elevons. The engines were of the much more powerful 200-series, the onboard systems were largely redesigned, and provision was made for carrying the Blue Steel cruise missile with a megaton-class thermonuclear warhead. Between 1960-65 Avro (or rather Hawker Siddeley) delivered 89 of this version. ▶

Below: No 44 Sqn's B.2s carried a stylised "44" and the arms of the City of Lincoln on their fins, their base being Waddington. The nose pimple is terrain-avoidance radar.

The Vulcan B.2 served with Nos 9, 12, 27, 35, 44, 50, 83, 101 and 617 Squadrons, setting an outstanding record and often bringing home trophies in various overseas competitions. During their long career they were upgraded to B.2A standard by being fitted with the even more powerful Olympus 301. Other visible changes included the fitting of augmented avionics, including extra tail ECM, a large flat-plate antenna group under the two right-hand jetpipes, and ARI.18228 radar warning in a flat box on top of the fin. From 1964 nuclear bombs and Blue Steel were withdrawn, and the Vulcans were dedicated to NATO as a conventional low-level force, painted in polyurethane grey/green camouflage and with TER (terrain-following radar) in a 'pimple' on the nose for missions at 500ft (152m) or even lower. FR (flight-refuelling) probes were removed, except from one group of aircraft of No 27 which, designated Vulcan SR.2, served in the maritime radar-reconnaissance role with extra fuel and various cameras and reconnaissance radar, for surveillance of large ocean areas.

The RAF planned to withdraw all Vulcans between June 1981 and June 1982, the only replacement being the smaller Tornado. In April 1982 a few were left when Operation Corporate was mounted to retake the Falklands (Argentina had previously tried to buy ex-RAF Vulcans). Within a matter of days the FR probes were tracked down and refitted, new Carousel inertial navigation systems were installed, pylons for Shrike anti-radar missiles were added beneath the wings and many other modifications were made. In a separate operation six aircraft were converted as K.2A tankers, with an FR hose-drum unit in the tailcone, replacing the ECM gear. These served with No 50 Squadron. In the course of the Falklands campaign Vulcans made five 'Black Buck' conventional bombing missions against the runway at Port Stanley airfield. Involving multiple inflight refuellings, these gruelling sorties were almost exactly 4,000 miles (6437km) each way, with no alternates or diversions. They were the longest bombing missions in the history of air warfare.

Above: A B.2 (XL320) at the start of its career, with Blue Steel "stand-off bomb" but lacking ECM and TFR avionics.

Below: Vulcans often participated in the Strategic Air Command bombing navigation competitions. Here a KC-135 is at far left, while a B-52 lands in the background.

31

Handley Page Victor

B.1, B.2 and K.2

Origin: Handley Page Ltd, UK (tanker versions rebuilt by Hawker Siddeley, now British Aerospace).

Type: Strategic bomber, later converted to air-refuelling tanker.

Engines: (B.1) four 11,000lb (4,990kg) thrust Armstrong Siddeley Sapphire 202 turbojets, (B.2) 17,250lb (7,932kg) thrust Rolls-Royce Conway 103 turbofans, (B.2R, SR.2, K.2) 20,600lb (9,344kg) thrust Conway 201 turbofans.

Dimensions: Span (B.1) 110ft (33.53m), (B.2 as built) 120ft (36.58m), (K.2) 117ft (35.66m); length 1114t 11in (35.3m); height (B.1) 28ft 1in (8.59m), (B.2) 30ft 1.5in (9.2m); wing area (B.1) 2,406sq ft (223.5m²), (B.2 as built) 2,597sq ft (241.3m²), (K.2) 2,200sq ft (204.4m²).

Weights: Empty (B.1) 79,000lb (35,834kg), (B.2) 91,000lb (41,277kg), (K.2) 110,310lb (50,037kg); maximum loaded (B.1) 180,000lb (81,650kg), (B.2) 233,000lb (101,150kg), (K.2) 238,000lb (107,957kg).

Performance: Maximum speed (B.1, B.2) 645mph (1,038km/h), (K.2) 610mph (982km/h); service ceiling (B.1) 55,000ft (16,764m), (B.2) 61,000ft (18,590m), (K.2) 50,000ft (15,240m); range (B.1, maximum bombload) 2,700 miles (4,345km), (B.2, maximum bombload) 4,600 miles, (K.2 not using transfer fuel) 4,000 miles (6,437km).

Armament: All bomber versions had internal provision for a range of nuclear or conventional bombs including 35 GP bombs of 1,000lb (454kg) nominal size; (B.2 and B.2R) provision for launching one Blue Steel Mk 1 cruise missile carried semi-externally; no defensive armament in any version; (tanker versions) none.

History: First flight (prototype) 24 December 1952; (production B.1) 1 February 1956; (B.2) 20 February 1959; (K.1 conversion) 28 April 1956, (K.2 conversion) 1 March 1972.

User: UK (RAF).

Deployment: In many respects the most efficient bomber of its era, the H.P.80 Victor was designed to Specification B.35/46, the same as the Vulcan. Though both aircraft had a totally different configuration the customer was never able to choose between them, and both were put into production and had long careers in the RAF. Basic features of the Handley Page bomber included a finely streamlined fuselage with a crew of five in the pressurized nose (only the pilots having ejection seats), a capacious bomb bay (which, together with two underwing pods which were never fitted, could have carried 63 bombs of 1,000lb), four engines buried at the rear of the roots of the graceful so-called 'crescent wing' (fed by shallow ducts from inlets in the leading edge), extremely neat main landing gears each with eight very small tyres which folded up into the wing immediately outboard of the engines, large door airbrakes on each side of the fuselage tailcone, and a striking T-tail at a time when such an arrangement was uncommon. Most of the structure was of a novel metal-sandwich type with a 'filling' of corrugated sheet or honeycomb, giving a very smooth external surface.

Only 50 Victor B.1s were built, serving with No 232 OCU (Operational Conversion Unit) and Nos 10, 15 and 57 Squadrons where they proved popular and set a enviable record of efficiency and safety. Almost all were later upgraded with flight-refuelling probes, large underwing tanks and enhanced ECM including a prominent array of antennas in the tailcone. This version, the B.1A, also served with No 55 Sqn. From 1961 the B.1A was joined in service by 30 Victor B.2 bombers, with almost double the power, extended wings and almost totally redesigned systems. The objective was an increase in over-target height, but by the late 1950s it was realized that future attacks would have to be made at low level. In any case, the availability of the massive Blue Steel stand-off missile enabled the bomber to turn back anything up to 200 ▶

Above: A B.2 bomber wends its way over the taxi track, probably at Marham or Wittering, in the mid-1960s.

Below: Surely among the most graceful aircraft ever built, XA918 was the second production B.1, powered by Sapphires. It had yet to collect underwing tanks, ECM protuberances, speed bumps, FR probe and other excrescences.

▶ miles (322km) from heavily defended targets. The B.2 served with RAF Nos 100 and 139 Sqn, and a third unit, No 543 Sqn, was equipped with the B/SR.2 strategic reconnaissance conversion with the whole belly occupied by cameras and SLAR (side-looking airborne radar). The B/SR.2 was able to make a detailed radar map of an area of 750,000 sq miles (1,492,500km²) in six hours. These impressive aircraft were withdrawn when No 543 Sqn disbanded in 1974, and since then Britain has had no strategic reconnaissance capability.

In 1965-67 surviving B.1A bombers were converted into K.1A air-refuelling tankers, the initial conversions being done in a panic to replace the grounded Valiants which had left the RAF with no tankers. At first, just two hose-drum units were fitted, one under each outer wing; later a third was added in the rear fuselage to permit three aircraft to be refuelled simultaneously. The K.1A served with Nos 55, 57 and 214 Sqns. From 1974 until 1977 these aircraft were progressively replaced by the Victor K.2, a complete rebuild which encountered major difficulties and required considerable new design work by British Aerospace at Woodford (the original Handley Page firm having gone bankrupt). Altogether, 24 B.2s were rebuilt, with 19 internal fuel tanks holding just 100,000lb (45,360kg) of fuel which can be transferred through three hose-drum units, one under each outer wing and the third in what had previously been the flash-bomb bay to the rear of the main bomb bay.

From early April 1982 almost the whole surviving force of Citor K.2s, consolidated into No 55 Sqn, was based at Wideawake airfield on Ascension Island. They bore the entire burden of the enormous air-refuelling task for C-130 and Vulcan aircraft, and the occasional Nimrod, shuttling to the Falkland Islands or patrolling the South Atlantic. These intensive missions consumed almost all the remaining life of the fatigued Victor airframes, and they were progressively withdrawn from early 1986 onwards.

Below: XH672, a B.2, is seen passing the signals square. Note the open ram-air turbine inlets above the fuselage.

Above: Sixteen main-gear tyres fold away as a B.2 gets airborne.
This was before conversion to carry Blue Steel.

Vickers-Armstrongs Valiant

Valiant BK.1

Origin: Vickers-Armstrongs (Aircraft) Ltd, UK.
Type: Strategic bomber with tanker capability.
Engines: Four 10,050lb (4,559kg) thrust Rolls-Royce Avon 205 turbojets.
Dimensions: Span 114ft 4in (34.85m); length (without flight refuelling probe) 108ft 3in (33m); height 32ft 2in (9.8m); wing area 2,362sq ft (219.44m²).
Weights: Empty 76,120lb (34,528kg); maximum loaded 175,000lb (79,380kg).
Performance: Maximum speed at high altitude 554mph (892km/h); cruising speed 495mph (797km/h); speed at sea level 414mph (662km/h); service ceiling 54,000ft (16,460m); range (with external fuel) 4,500 miles (7,242km).
Armament: Internal bay for various nuclear bombs or up to 21 GP bombs of 1,000lb (454kg) size; no defensive armament.
History: First flight (prototype) 18 May 1951, (production B.1) 21 December 1953, (last production aircraft) 27 August 1957; withdrawal from service January 1965.
User: UK (RAF).

Below: This B(PR)K.1 multi-role aircraft shows the white anti-flash paint scheme. Note the Bloodhound SAMs.

Deployment: Though it gained little publicity, the Valiant was perhaps Britain's most successful programme for a military aircraft since World War II. Designed and developed under intense pressure, it did more than was asked of it, sustained a production run of 107 aircraft all delivered early and within budget, and gave outstanding service until, having been thrust into the unforeseen low-level role, the structure showed fatigue cracks. Back in 1953, Vickers had flown a single Valiant B.2 with an airframe stressed for low-level missions, and with speed at sea level increased to 552mph (888km/h). Ironically, this was not the version ordered into production. A clear case of shortsightedness.

Above: WB215 was the second prototype, flown in April 1952. It was bright polished metal all over.

► The Vickers Type 660 Valiant had originally been designed to Specification B.9/48, conceived as an interim requirement and less challenging than the B.35/46 document which led to the Vulcan and Victor. The idea was that, being slightly less demanding, a bomber could be produced to B.9/48 quite quickly and rushed into service while the other V-bombers' were still under development, despite it being started later. The design team at Weybridge performed wonders to get the prototype in the air so quickly, though it was lost in January 1952 from inflight fire. Its features included a high-mounted modestly swept wing, with the four engines buried in the roots and fed from leading-edge inlets, a crew of five housed in the pressurized forward fuselage (the front pressure bulkhead being of concave shape to make room for the big nav/bombing radar in the nose), a large bomb bay under the wing, fully powered flight controls, and main landing gears comprising twin tandem legs electrically retracted outwards into the wing. Altogether, the Valiant was a good compromise between the conflicting demands of high performance and low risk.

During 1951-53 the Type 660 was developed into the production Type 706, or Valiant B.1, with more powerful Avon engines fed through enlarged inlets, greatly enhanced systems, the nav/bombing radar and a ventral visual bombing position, an extended tailcone planned to house ECM (electronic countermeasures) equipment and provision for rocket assisted take off (not used in service), and large drop tanks under the wings. Five pre-production aircraft were followed by 20 production machines, deliveries to the RAF No 230 OCU beginning in autumn 1954. Interspersed with B.1s were 11 dual-role B (PR).1s able to fly bombing or reconnaissance missions with No 543 Squadron. Also interspersed in the B.1 line were 14 even more versatile aircraft. Designated B(PR)K.1, these were able to operate as high-level bombers, or with the multi-sensor reconnaissance pallet of the B(PR) or with an inflight-refuelling hose-drum unit installed in the rear of the bomb-bay together with extra internal fuel. At the end of the variegated B.1 line came a straight run of 48 aircraft designated BK.1, operating either as bombers or as air-refuelling tankers. By 1957 these completed the run of 104 production Valiants.

Valiants were initially delivered painted silver, with black numbers. By 1957 they were painted in anti-flash white for nuclear attacks, with pale blue/pink roundels and pale markings. The crews were equipped with special anti-flash vizors. Early B.1s dropped ordinary HE bombs in anger when they were called upon to attack targets in Egypt during the Suez campaign in November 1956.

Below: Feverish activity at Wittering as a B(PR).1 of 138 Sqn is readied for a night mission. Note the huge radar.

On 11 October 1956, aircraft WZ366 of No 49 Squadron released Britain's first air-dropped nuclear weapon over Maralinga, Australia, and in Operation 'Grapple' on 15 May 1957 XD818 dropped the first (and only) British air-dropped thermonuclear 'H-bomb' over Malden Island in the central Pacific.

Valiants served with RAF Nos 7, 18, 49, 90, 138, 148, 199, 207, 214 and 543 Squadrons. They were extremely popular, but increasingly found themselves acting in the tanker role — they were the only aircraft in the RAF able to air-refuel both fighter and V-bomber squadrons on long overseas deployments. From 1962, it was belatedly recognised that future bombers would have to fly at the lowest possible altitude if they were to escape radar detection and almost certain destruction when penetrating hostile airspace. The remaining Valiants were therefore painted in low-level camouflage and formed into a tactical wing based at Marham and assigned to SACEUR (Supreme Allied Commander, Europe) as part of the defence of NATO. Unfortunately, as the airframes had never been designed for low-level operations, they quickly developed dangerous fatigue cracks. These were first noticed in August 1964, and in January 1965 the entire force was grounded. This precipitated a crisis in the RAF because it left Britain's air arm with no tankers.

Below: WZ400 was an all-can-do B(PR)K.1, seen here at low level but still painted white (but with black serial number, the anti-flash livery normally having pale numbers).

Boeing B-52 Stratofortress

B-52D, G and H

Origin: Boeing Airplane Company, Seattle, Washington (today Boeing Military Airplane Company, Wichita, Kansas).

Type: Heavy bomber and missile platform.

Engines: Eight Pratt & Whitney jet engines, (B-52D) 12,100lb (5,489kg) thrust J57-29W turbojets, (G) 13,750lb (6,237kg) thrust J57-43W turbojets, (H) 17,000lb (7,711kg) thrust TF33-3 turbofans.

Dimensions: Span 185ft (56.39m); length (D, and G/H as built) 157ft 7in (48m), (G/H today) 160ft 11in (49.05m); height (D) 48ft 4½in (14.7m), (G/H) 40ft 8in (12.4m); wing area 4,000sq ft (371.6m²).

Weights: Empty (D) 176,000lb (79,834kg), (G/H) 195,000lb (88,450kg); maximum take-off (D) 470,000lb (213,200kg), (G/H) 505,000lb (229,000kg); maximum after inflight refuelling (H only) 566,000lb (256,738kg).

Performance: Maximum speed at high altitude (D) 575mph (925km/h), (G/H) 595mph (957km/h); maximum combat penetration speed at low altitude (all) 405mph (652km/h); typical cruising speed at high altitude (all) 509mph (Mach 0.77, 819km/h); service ceiling (D) 45,000ft (13,700m), (G) 46,000ft (14,000m), (H) 47,000ft (14,300m); take-off run on full-range mission (D) 11,100ft (3,383m), (G) 10,000ft (3,050m), (H) 9,500ft (2,895m); range (maximum fuel, high-altitude cruise, no external weapons) (D) 7,370 miles (11,861km), (G) 8,406 miles (13,528km), (H) 10,130 miles (16,303km).

Armament: (D) internal bay for 84 bombs of nominal 500lb plus pylons under the inboard wings for 24 bombs of nominal 750lb for actual total weight of about 89,000lb (40,370kg), with defensive armament comprising four 0.5in guns in radar-directed tail turret; (G) internal bay for eight nuclear bombs (several varieties) or eight SRAM missiles on rotary dispenser, plus wing pylons for either 12 SRAM missiles or 12 ALCM cruise missiles, with defensive armament comprising four 0.5in guns in remote-controlled tail barbette, (G, Maritime Support) eight or 12 AGM-84D Harpoon anti-ship missiles to be fitted with CSRL (Common Strategic Rotary Launcher) able to accept eight SRAMs, ALCMs or advanced cruise missiles, and to be fitted with wing pylons for 12 SRAMs or ALCMs, with defensive armament comprising one 20mm T171 six-barrelled cannon in tail 'stinger'.

History: First flight 15 April 1952; first delivery to SAC (RB-52B) 29 June 1955; final delivery (H) 26 October 1963.

User: USA (AF).

Deployment: A legend in its own lifetime, the B-52 already has a history that has extended four times as long as that originally planned. Moreover, the B-52G and H will continue in combat service probably until the end of the century. At first, the B-52 project was for a turboprop, because in 1948-49 there was no way a jet bomber could meet the long-range requirements of the SAC missions without unacceptably frequent inflight refuelling. The breakthrough came with the Pratt & Whitney J57, a high-compression turbojet offering improved fuel economy and sufficient power for an eight-engined bomber to ►

Above: This B-52G was used in May 1979 to test carriage and separation of dummy AGM-86 cruise missiles.

Below: First take-off with dummy Boeing ALCMs in May 1979. The aircraft was B-52G No 587-204.

meet all requirements. In great urgency the B-52 was designed in 1950-51 to carry up to four nuclear bombs at high altitude over ranges of about 7,000 miles. Features included four twin-jet pods slung under the giant but flexible wings, four twin-wheel landing-gear trucks which could be steered or slewed in unison to facilitate cross-wind landings, a pressurized nose compartment for five, including two pilots seated side-by-side as in earlier US bombers, a manned tail turret with gunlaying radar, unprecedented fuel capacity in both fuselage and wings, and a receptacle for 'Flying Boom' refuelling.

Early deliveries included RB-52 reconnaissance versions in which the weapons bay was occupied by a pressurized capsule housing two operators and various cameras and electronic reconnaissance gear, but these had a short life in service. Boeing's Seattle factory was soon joined in the programme by that at Wichita, and in the late 1950s output reached 20 per month, as well as 20 KC-135 tankers per month to support the SAC bombers. Each successive version introduced new features, the biggest single change coming with the B-52G, first flown on 26 October 1958. This was the first version to have 'wet' integral-tankage wings without separate fuel cells (giving increased capacity),

Below: A B-62G, without cruise missile pylons but with all the latest avionics upgrades, manoeuvres into position to take fuel from a KC-135 of the Utah Air National Guard. The right rear landing-gear door is open.

Above: The tall-finned, black-painted B-52D was the chief carrier of ''iron bombs'' in the war against North Vietnam.

Below: The B-52G pictured on p.41 is seen here with ALQ-153 tail-warning radar and carrying AGM-69A SRAM missiles.

43

as well as structural changes, a shorter vertical tail and a revised crew arrangement which relocated the tail gunner in the forward fuselage. By the late 1950s the ADM-20 Quail was often being carried. This was a pilotless miniature aircraft constructed mainly of plastics and fitted with a J85 turbojet and electronic devices to give it a signature on hostile radars identical to that of a B-52. Another new load comprised two AGM-28 Hound Dog cruise missiles carried on wing pylons, but both Quail and Hound Dog were eventually withdrawn. In the final version, which brought total deliveries up to 744 aircraft, the B-52H introduced the TF33 trubofan engine, which greatly increased flight performance (notably range) and eliminated the need for water injection on take off.

During the Vietnam war, the B-52D and B-52F saw much action, initially on gruelling 12-hour missions from Andersen AFB, Guam. The F could carry only the original load of 27 bombs of 500lb or 750lb, use of conventional bombs having been given little attention in the original B-52 design. The B-52D, however, was subjected to a major rebuild to enable it to carry greatly increased loads

Meanwhile, the G and H versions were subjected to a series of major update programmes which are continuing to this day and have already cost several times the original purchase price of the aircraft. These programmes have included structural strengthening for sustained flight at low altitudes, the addition of AGM-69A SRAMs, the EVS (electro-optical viewing system) which added twin chin bulges and big pilot displays to facilitate low-level flight at night or in bad weather, cartridge starters for a quick getaway from a threatened airfield, new threat-warning systems, smart noise jammers, the CMI (cruise-missile interface), a satellite link and, most costly of all, the extensive OAS (offensive avionics system) to enhance the ability of the bombers to survive in ► hostile airspace.

Below: A B-52G, No 58-0170, with all the latest avionics updates including the Offensive Avionics System. It is carrying real AGM-86B cruise missiles and has ''strakelets''.

► A total of 99 B-52Gs have been rebuilt to carry the AGM-86B cruise missile, both internally (eight, on the rotary launcher) and externally (12). The remaining 69 of the G-model are being equipped with Harpoon anti-ship missiles for use in the Maritime Support role. An alternative weapon for these aircraft is the GBU-15(V) precision-guided stand-off weapon for use against either ship or shore targets. The 96 surviving B-52H bombers are now in the process of conversion to carry AGM—86Bs and whatever later advanced cruise missile may be ordered. After being equipped with the ICSM (integrated conventional stores management) system, the G and H bombers are expected to serve at least until the year 2000.

Right: The last and most powerful version was the B-52H, powered by TF33 turbofans. This example was photographed before the many avionics update programmes.

Below right: A B-52G on final approach at a SAC base. At this time these aircraft (58-0225 is nearest) had not been converted to carry cruise missiles.

Below: One of the final batch of B-52Gs, No 59-2580, depicted at low level while engaged in exercise William Tell 80. At this time CM conversion had not begun.

Dassault Mirage IV

Mirage IVA, IVP

Origin: Avions Marcel Dassault (now Dassault-Breguet), France.
Type: Strategic bomber and missile carrier.
Engines: Two 15,432lb (7,000kg) thrust SNECMA Atar 09K afterburning turbojets (thrust given is at sea level with maximum afterburner).
Dimensions: Span 38ft 10.5in (11.85m); length 77ft 1in (23.5m); height 17ft 8.7in (5.41m); wing area 839.6sq ft (78m²).
Weights: Empty (A) 31,967lb (14,500kg), (P) 32,900lb (14,925kg); maximum loaded, about 73,800lb (33,475kg).
Performance: Maximum speed (dash, high altitude) 1,454mph (Mach 2.2, 2,340km/h) at 40,000ft (12,190m); maximum speed (sustained, high altitude) 1,222mph (Mach 1.7, 1,966km/h) at 60,000ft (18,288m); crusing speed (also maximum speed at low level) 595mph (958km/h); service ceiling, just over 60,000ft (18,500m); combat radius without inflight refuelling (hi-lo-hi, dash in target area) 770 miles (1,240km); ferry range 2,485 miles (4,000km).
Armament: (A) One AN22 free-fall nuclear bomb, usually of 60kT (kilotonnes) yield, or up to 16,000lb (7,258kg) of conventional weapons on external pylons; no defensive armament; (P) one ASMP nuclear cruise missile.
History: First flight (prototype) 17 June, (production IVA) 7 December 1963, (IVP conversion) May 1985, following ASMP trials on modified IVA in June 1983.
User: France (Armée de l'Air).

Deployment: Together with the successive versions of silo-launched SSBS and submarine-launched MSBS ballistic missiles, the MIrage IVA has, since 1965, been a delivery system of the French nuclear deterrent. France is the only country other than the two superpowers to have such a 'triad' of nuclear delivery systems. The bombers are assigned to the CFAS (Commandement des Forces Aériennes Stratégique), forming a so-called *Force De Dissuasion,* or deterrent force. Because of their small size they rely heavily on in-flight refuelling, and their basing is flexible and well adapted to dispersion in the event of a crisis.

The Mirage IVA is aerodynamically similar to the Mirage III fighter, with a 60° delta wing and trailing-edge elevons mounted low on a slim fuselage with lateral inlets with axially sliding half-cone centrebodies to adjust the inlet to subsonic or supersonic flight. Compared with the fighter, however, the bomber is considerably larger, has two engines (of very similar type), a crew of two in tandem cockpits, four-wheel bogie main landing gears and totally different avionics and systems including a complex radar navigation and bombing system. In the nose is the flight-refuelling probe. The missions were planned using aircraft in pairs, one carrying a bomb and the other an overload of fuel and a 'buddy' hose-drum refuelling unit with which it could top up its companion to enable it to fly its mission. Alternatively, tanker support can be furnished by the C-135FR tankers of the Armée de l'Air, but these would not usually assist on a combat mission. Even with tanker support, many missions have been planned either on a no-return basis or on the assumption that recovery would be made to friendly territory nearer to the target.

The total procurement comprised 62 aircraft, which at first were assigned to three *Escadres* (wings), the 91st at Mont de Marsan, the 93rd at Istres and the 94th at Avord. Each of these was in turn divided into three groups of four aircraft, two at combat readiness and two dispersed away from base. To assist dispersal provision was made to attach eight rockets under the inboard wings, enabling the laden aircraft to take off from short strips hardened by spraying quick-setting chemicals on the soil. Today, most of the 62 aircraft have been withdrawn from bomber duty. One group of 12 have been rebuilt as Mirage IVR ▶

Above: Aerodynamically the Mirage IVA is probably the "cleanest" bomber ever built, especially from this aspect.

Below: One of the first trials with the formidable battery of solid-fuel take-off booster rockets, for STOL getaway.

▶ reconnaissance aircraft, possessing no weapon capability but equipped with comprehensive EW (electronic-warfare) systems, cameras, IR (infra-red) linescan and a side-looking airborne radar. Some of the larger sensors are packaged in a large external pod.

Since the 1970s France (mainly Aérospatiale) has been developing an impressive stand-off missile, ASMP *(air-sol moyenne portée,* or air/ground long range). With a range of at least 62 miles (100km) at highly supersonic speed, this carries a warhead of 100 or 150kT, with its own self-contained navigation system which can programme the missile to execute dog-legs and evasive manoeuvres. To deliver ASMRs, a batch of 18 Mirage IVA bombers has been gutted and completely upgraded to IVP *(Pénétration)* standard. The IVP has a Thomson-CSF Arcana pulse-doppler radar, dual inertial navigation systems, a Thomson-CSF electronic jamming pod and Matra Phimat chaff-dispensing pod (on the two outboard pylons), two 440gal (528US gallons, 2000-litre) drop tanks on the inboard pylons, and a new RWR (radar-warning receiver) installation. The Mirage IVP first entered service in 1986 with EB 1/91 Gascogne, followed by 2/91 Bretagne. No other country outside the superpowers has the capability to make supersonic strategic attacks, followed by delivery of a supersonic cruise missile. The Mirage IVP, together with the IVR, will remain in front-line duty at least until the end of the century, but the original Mirage IVA force is progressively being run down.

Right: A Mirage IVP launching an ASMP cruise missile. The Mirage IVA carries conventional weapons or one nuclear bomb.

Below: Looking up at a pre-camouflaged IVA one can see the circular radome and the large recess for the AN22 bomb. Today the ASMP cruise missile can be carried.

General Dynamics
FB-111A

FB-111A

Origin: General Dynamics Corporation, Fort Worth, Texas.
Type: Two-seat bomber with Mach 2 capability.
Engines: Two 20,350lb (9,231kg) thrust Pratt & Whitney TF30-7
augmented turbofans (thrust given is at sea level with full augmentation).
Dimensions: Span (wings swept 16°) 70ft (21.34m), (wings swept 72.5°)
33ft 11in (10.34m); length 73ft 6in (22.4m); height 17ft (5.18m); wing area
555sq ft (51.56m²).
Weights: Empty 49,700lb (22,544kg); maximum loaded 114,300lb
(51,846kg).
Performance: Maximum speed at high altitude (no external stores)
1,320mph (Mach 2, 2,124km/h); penetration cruising speed 571mph
(919km/h); take-off run at 100,000lb weight 4,700ft (1,433m); service ceiling
(afterburner) 52,000ft (15,850m); range with external fuel 4,100l miles
(6,600km).
Armament: Internal bay for two B43 or B83 nuclear bombs or up to two
supersonic AGM-69A SRAMs (Short-Range Attack Missile) or bombs of
750lb nominal size; two swivelling pylons under each wing for total of four
AGM-69As or up to 24 bombs of 750lb nominal size; structural provision for
two further pylons under each outer wing, non-swivelling and usable only
with wings at 16° sweep, designed for 24 more 750lb bombs or similar loads
(these pylons have never been fitted in service).
History: First flight 13 July 1968; first delivery to SAC (340th Bomb Group,
a training unit at Carswell AFB) 8 October 1969.
User: USA (AF).

**Right: Looking up at an FB-111A with the doors to the internal bay
open, showing an AGM-69A SRAM (the streamlined white store on
the left-hand side). Two can be carried.**

**Below: An FB-111A dropping a SRAM over the White Sands missile
range. In a moment the rocket will ignite.**

Deployment: Planned as the TFX (Tactical Fighter, Experimental) in 1959, the F-111 proved to be one of the most controversial aircraft in history. This was partly because of arguments over which bidder (General Dynamics or Boeing) should be selected, partly because it was claimed the inferior submission was picked at the higher price, partly because the current Defense Secretary insisted the project be combined with a Navy requirement — a common airplane being developed for both services — and partly because the initial production F-111A proved to have little capability in the fighter role and suffered from worse escalation in weight, engine/airframe mismatch problems and structural failure of any aircraft of recent times. Eventually, the F-111 matured as an outstanding tactical attack aircraft of the USAF Tactical Air Command and USAFE, pioneering today's essential technique of automatic terrain following at the lowest possible safe level in order to minimise detection by defending radars and SAM systems. The original F-111A was combat-proven in Vietnam, where its highly professional crews, each comprising a pilot and navigator seated side-by-side, proved that with skill and iron nerve a terrain-following attack can even be made through mountainous country at night or in cloud.

In most essentials the FB-111A resembles the F-111 tactical attack family of aircraft, with twin augmented turbofan engines, a high-mounted wing with the main panels pivoted well outboard of the fuselage (so that sweep angle can be adjusted in flight between 16° for take off and landing and 72.5° for a supersonic dash), and extremely large main gears pivoted to the fuselage which, together with a large door-type airbrake, make the underside of the fuselage unavailable for carrying stores except for ECM pods. In the nuclear role SRAMs or bombs would be carried internally, the four wing pylons being used to carry drop tanks. In the conventional role the wing pylons would be fitted with long TERs (triple ejector racks), with no room for external fuel.

The main changes from the tactical versions are extended wingtips, strengthened landing fear, a slightly more powerful TF30 engine, SRAM provisions and revised avionics for extended-range missions, the main radar being the APQ-114 and a doppler radar and astrocompass being added. The original ►

▶ plan in 1965 was that SAC should procure 210 aircraft, which would serve as replacements for the B-58 force and for the B-52 versions up to the F. A further 53 FB-111As were to be bought as spares and to make good attrition losses. Rapidly rising prices reduced the eventual purchase to only 76 aircraft, barely sufficient to support two active wings. Deliveries originally went to the 340th Bomb Group, the 4007th Combat Crew Training Squadron and the 4201st Test Squadron. Since the mid-1970s, however, the two combat units have been the 380th Bomb Wing at Plattsburgh, New York, and the 509th Bomb Wing at Pease AFB in New Hampshire.

In service, the FB-111A — which is usually not dubbed 'the Aardvark', as are the tactical versions — has proved popular with its crews and has set an exemplary record in nearly all respects. Crews from the 509th Bomb Wing in particular have recently tended to take the top trophies in the annual SAC bombing and navigation competition, closely rivalled by the 380th, though with the B-1B now in service this pattern may be expected to change. The FB has not served overseas nor dropped weapons in anger. Almost all simulated attacks are made at low level at speeds of around 570mph (917km/h), tough it is becoming increasingly important to conserve structural life and avoid costly fatigue damage.

When they were ordered in the mid-1960s the various F-111 versions were in many ways representative of the latest thinking, but their vital avionics were often 'off the shelf' and chosen primarily for reasons of availability and reliability (which were often not achieved). In October 1986 General Dynamics began a giant six-year programme which will completely gut and re-equip all 381 aircraft in the USAF front-line inventory, including the FBs, which will receive new main and terrain-following radars, warning and countermeasure systems and communications and cockpit displays.

Above: The FT-111A was able to meet SAC mission requirements by carrying up to 3,000 US gal (13,638 lit) of external fuel.

Below: FB-111A No 68-0264 is seen here on a simulated combat mission during Exercise Global Shield 1979.

Ilyushin Il-28 Beagle and H-5

Il-28R

Origin: The S.V. Ilyushin OKB, Soviet Union; also built by state factory in Csechoslovakia and Harbin Aircraft Manufacturing Corporation, China.

Type: Tactical bomber, reconnaissance aircraft and trainer.

Engines: two 5,952lb (2,700kg) thrust Klimov VK-1A turbojets.

Dimensions: Span (excluding tip tanks) 70ft 4.5in (21.45m); length (excluding tail guns) 57ft 11in (17.65m); height 21ft 11.8in (6.7m); wing area 654.45sq ft (60.8m²).

Weights: Empty (typical) 28,417lb (12,890kg); maximum loaded 46,738lb (21,200kg).

Performance: Maximum speed, 500mph (805km/h) at 39,370ft (12,000m), 560mph (902km/h) at 14,760ft (4,500m) and 497mph (800km/h) at sea level; cruising speed (typical, medium altitudes) 478mph (770km/h); service ceiling 40,350ft (12,350m); range (maximum fuel) 1,490 miles (2,400km) at 267mph (430km/h) at high altitude, 705 miles (1,135km) at 472mph (760km/h) at low level.

Armament: Internal bay for up to 6,614lb (3,000kg) of bombs, mines, depth charges or two 45-36A torpedoes, original Il-28 and H-5 being configured to carry a nuclear weapon; two fixed NR-23 23mm cannon firing ahead and two similar guns in K-6 manned tail turret. Il-28R/HZ-5 retains guns only, and Il-28U/HJ-5 has no armament.

History: First flight 8 July 1948; first regiment equipped September 1950; Chinese production 1966-82.

User: Soviet Union and 21 other countries.

Deployment The powerful Ilyushin OKB (experimental aircraft bureau), which had already designed and flown the Il-22 four-jet bomber, began the design of a light tactical bomber in December 1947. Work proceded with incredible speed, in order to compete against the rival Su-10 and various Tupolev (Tu) prototypes. The key to the design was the availability of the British Rolls-Royce Nene engine, used as the RD-45 in the prototype in a nacelle very similar to the underwing nacelles of the Tu bombers, and housing the retracted main gears with the wheel turned through 90° to lie flat under the rear of the engine, where it joined the long jetpipe extending well aft of the wing. The wing was unswept and, like the circular-section fuselage, was made in halves (upper/lower for the wing, left/right for the fuselage). When fully equipped with systems and equipment, the halves were joined together. The tail surfaces were swept back to avoid any control problems at the maximum diving speed.

The bomb-bay occupied the lower part of the centre fuselage, with a large rubber fuel tank ahead of it, another above the front section (ahead of the wing spars) and a third large tank in the rear fuselage. No fuel was put in the wing. In the nose of the pressurized crew compartment was the navigator/bombardier, with an ejection seat and both optical and radar systems for navigation and bomb aiming (the optical set being derived from the American Norden M-9). Immediately behind, on the centreline, sat the pilot, under a fighter-type canopy hinged to the right and jettisoned prior to ejection. In the tail was a pressurized compartment for a gunner manning the K-6 turret, with a ventral escape hatch. No crew member could leave his seat. Flight controls were all manual, but the Il-28 proved surprisingly manoeuvrable. When, in October 1948, Marshal Vershinin ordered three test crews to evaluate it against the bigger Tu-78, all three voted for the Ilyushin.

Large-scale production ensued, the basic Il-28 bomber (given the NATO reporting name of 'Butcher', later changed to 'Beagle') being followed on the assembly lines by the Il-28R reconnaissance aircraft (with a camera-filled

Above: One of the long-time operators of the I1-28 was Finland's Ilmavoimat (air force). Though simple, this bomber was popular with its crews, partly because of its reliability, good handling and almost complete absence of vices.

bomb-bay and fitted with tip tanks), the I1-28T torpedo bomber for the AV-MF (naval air force), the I1-28U pilot trainer (with no armament or radar and seating just the pilot and instructor in tandem stepped cockpits with dual controls), and the I1-20 unarmed transport for Aeroflot (used for urgent cargo such as newspaper printing matrices). Total deliveries have been estimated at 3,000, plus at least 200 built in Czechoslovakia as the B-228. Of this total over 1,500 were exported to 15 countries including all members of the Warsaw Pact. The I1-28 proved popular and easy to maintain, and has seen action in more conflicts than any other jet bomber, including NIgeria and Biafra, Egypt, Vietnam, North Korea, Iraq, Yemen, Syria and probably Afghanistan. In most of these operations it was used as a level bomber from fairly low altitude. It did not prove wholly suitable to precision attacks on point targets, except using the forward guns.

During the past 20 years the I1-28 has been of the greatest importance to China. The People's Republic received large numbers from the Soviet Union, and from 1966 began manufacturing the aircraft, with small changes, as the H-5 (Hongzhaji 5, bomber No 5). The Harbin factory delivered about 500 by 1982. Three versions were built, designated H-5 (bomber), HZ-5 (reconnaissance) and HJ-5 (trainer). The WP-5D engines, also made in the Harbin complex, are virtually identical to the VK-1A turbojets, but the aircraft's equipment and instruments differ in many respects from the Soviet original. The bomber version is equipped to carry torpedoes, and a small number were exported, including a batch to Albania. H-5s of the Chinese Navy are equipped to tow Rushton modified low-level targets bought from Britain in 1985 to simulate sea-skimming missiles. The HZ-5, which like the other versions serves with both the People's Liberation Army and Navy, has been updated to carry various alternative palletized loads including cameras, IR linescan and various electronic-intelligence sensors, including some installations purchased from Western countries. These aircraft are likely to remain in service into the 1990s.

Myasishchyev M-4 Bison

M-4 Bison-A, B, C

Origin: The OKB of Professor V.M. Myasishchyev, Soviet Union.
Type: Designed as strategic bomber, later converted as air-refuelling tanker and maritime reconnaissance aircraft.
Engines: All production versions, four 19,180lb (8,700kg) thrust Mikulin Am-3D turbojets, later replaced by 20,943lb (9,500kg) thrust AM-3M.
Dimensions: Span 165ft 7.4in (50.48m); length (A) 154ft 10in (47.2m), (B) 162ft 6¼in (49.54m), (C) given as 175ft 2.3in (53.4m), though this appears excessive; height 46ft (14.24m); wing area 3,400sq ft (320m²).
Weights: Empty (A) 185,000lb (83,900kg), (C) 198,500lb (90,000kg); maximum loaded (A) 352,730lb (160,000kg), (C, overload) 462,963lb (210,000kg).
Performance: Maximum speed (all, high altitude) 560mph (900km/h), (sea level) 385mph (620km/h); typical cruising speed (high altitude) 519mph (835km/h); service ceiling (160 tonnes) 52,000ft (15,850m); range (A, high altitude, 12,000lb/5,450kg bombload) 6,650 miles (10,700km), (A, maximum bombload) 4,970 miles (8,000km), (C, overload fuel) 18,000km (11,000 miles).
Armament: (A, as built) internal bay for up to four thermonuclear bombs or 33,070lb (15,000kg) of conventional bombs, with defensive armament of 10, NR-23 23mm cannon in tail, and front and rear dorsal and ventral remote-controlled barbettes; (A, today) as before, with rear dorsal and ventral barbettes removed; (B, C) as A, but with bomb-bay occupied by other installations.
History: First flight late 1953; service delivery (A) 1956.
User: Soviet Union (VVS, AV-MF).

Deployment: In its day, this giant four-jet bomber represented an outstanding aerodynamic and structural technical achievement. Indeed, the original aircraft have remained in service for over 30 years with flight times probably between 5,000 and 15,000 hours. Thanks to the availability of the

massive AM-3 powerplant this bomber was comparable to early versions of the eight-engined B-52, though it was never quite able to meet the severe range requirements of the VVS-ADD (long-range avaiation). The engines are almost the same as those fitted to the Tu-16 'Badger', and all four are buried inside the rear of the wing roots, fed by individual ducts from leading-edge inlets and with the engines and jetpipes splayed outwards to reduce buffet and noise fatigue on the rear fuselage. The circular-section fuselage houses the flight crew (usually five in the bomber) in a pressurized compartment, an enormous quantity of fuel ahead of, above and behind the bomb-bay, the front and rear four-wheel trucks of the landing gear and a small pressurized compartment for the tail gunner. On the tips of the slender swept wings are twin-wheel outrigger gears which fold forward into streamlined pods. These pods show in their nose-down attitude the remarkable washout (twist to remove incidence) of the outer wings. The wings house additional fuel and, when all tanks are filled, the tip gears press on the ground.

The emergence of this enormous jet bomber caused a ripple of fear in Washington. Codenamed 'Bison', it was responsible for most of the pressure that led to increasing the rate of manufacture of the B-52 and its supporting KC-135 tanker. Curiously, the large number of Bisons expected by ▶

Above: An M-4 of the ''Bison-B'' maritime reconnaissance type, photographed by a fighter of the Royal Air Force.

Below: The crew of six leave a Myasishchyev improved maritime reconnaissance aircraft of the type dubbed ''Bison-C'' by NATO. The user service is the AV-MF naval aviation.

► Washington never materialized, though as the 'Molot' (hammer), the aircraft received plenty of publicity in its homeland. One example was refitted with Soloviev D-15 two-spool turbojets of 28,660lb (13,000kg) thrust. In 1959, with a crew of six, this aircraft lifted a payload of 121,480lb (55,220kg) to 6,561ft (2000m) and 22,050lb (10,000kg) to 50,253ft (15,317m). Again, it is surprising that this much more powerful version never went into production. This prototype was designated the 201-M. Another M-4, with unspecified engines, set a 621-mile (1000km) circuit record with a 59,524lb (27,000kg) payload at 638.77mph (1028km/h), well above the normal service maximum speed.

In the late 1950s, all 'Bison-A' bombers were fitted with an FR (flight-refuelling) probe above the glazed nose, and with upgraded EW systems (which have probably been progressively upgraded since). Others were converted as 'Bison-B' reconnaissance aircraft, with dual capability as air-refuelling tankers. The rear upper and lower barbettes were removed, a big radar put into the previously glazed nose and numerous sensors added, resulting in antennas, bumps and blisters in many places. Other M-4s were more extensively rebuilt as 'Bison-C' maritime reconnaissance aircraft which, like the B version, were assigned to the AV-MF. The C variant had an extended and pointed nose filled with electronics, with observation windows under the flight deck and the FR probe relocated at the tip of the nose. Small numbers have roamed far over oceanic areas, often showing individual features especially in the matter of avionics antennas.

Since 1980, the B and C reconnaissance versions have been replaced by 'Backfires', and the only M-4s believed to be in current service comprise about 43 of the bomber version and 31 of the air-refuelling tankers. The latter have a hose-drum unit in a bulged centre section of the bomb-bay, as in the dual-role reconnaissance versions, and some have been reported with two further hose-drum units under the outer wings. The tankers are used to support both the M-4 bombers and various types of Tu-95/Tu-142 'Bear'. A single M-4 of the Bison-C type has been modified to act as the carrier for initial flight testing of the Soviet 'space shuttle' orbiter. Apart from the dorsal interface cradle to carry the orbiter on its back, the main modification was to fit a completely new twin-finned tail unit with rectangular end-plate fins and rudders.

Above: An M-4 of the "Bison-B" type being escorted near the UK by a Lightning of RAF No 74 Sqn.

Below: One of the most recent photographs of an M-4, this shows a "Bison-C" type. Most survivors are tankers or bombers.

Northrop ATB

B-2 ?

Origin: Northrop Corporation Aircraft Group, Hawthorne/Palmdale, California.

Type: Low-observability 'stealth' bomber.

Engines: Believed to be two modified General Electric F101 turbofans, probably without augmentation and thus each rated at about 20,000lb (9,000kg), thrust.

Dimensions: Not disclosed, but span probably about 155ft (47.2m); length about 66ft (20m); height possibly as little as 15ft (4.5m); wing area, about 3,000sq ft (279m²).

Weights: Empty, probably about 150,000lb (68,000kg); maximum loaded, said to be in 400,000lb (181,440kg) class.

Performance: Maximum speed (over wide range of heights from seal level upwards) about Mach 0.85, equivalent to 647mph (1,040km/h) at sea level and to 560mph (900km(h) at high altitudes; combat ceiling, probably at least 50,000ft (15,240m); range on typical combat mission,with maximum bombload, said to be 5,758 miles (5,000 nautical miles, 9,262km).

Armament: Internal bay(s) for thermonuclear or conventional bombs, AGM-69A SRAM defence-suppression missiles, AGM-86B cruise missiles, General Dynamics advanced stealth cruise missiles, bombs containing advanced non-nuclear explsoives (SPH, spin-polarized hydrogen or MSH, metastable hydrogen) and other stores up to a total weight of 40,000lb (18,144kg); no guns will be carried, but an ASDL (airborne self-defence laser) might be installed.

History: First flight (proof-of-concept vehicle) said to have been 1982, (B-2) probably late 1988; initial operational capability, possible 1991.

User: USA (AF).

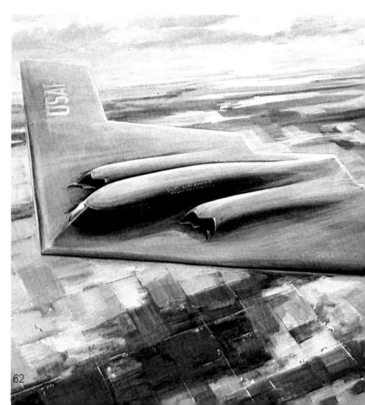

Deployment: In 1980 President Carter, and his Secretary of Defense, Dr Harold S. Brown, concluded that after 1990 the B-1 bomber would not be able to penetrate most Soviet defences with an acceptable degree of certainty. From 1973 a far-reaching research programme called Have Blue had both confirmed the vital necessity of future attack aircraft having low observability, or 'stealth' characteristics, and shown in broad outline how such characteristics could be achieved. As a result, it was decided to launch a programme for a totally new strategic bomber with the fullest possible stealth qualities, to enter service in the early 1990s as the future vehicle of USAF Strategic Air Command against the most heavily defended targets.

RFPs (requests for proposals) were issued in 1981 and elicited two major replies, one by a Rockwell/Lockheed partnership and the other by Northrop/Boeing. The former proposed a greatly enlarged derivative of the RA-19 reconnaissance/strike aircraft which is already in service with the USAF and which, despite having no afterburners, can cruise at supersonic speed. The team of Northrop and Boeing Military Airplane Company proposed a subsonic aircraft of essentially all-wing configuration, not greatly different in its essentials from Northrop's great XB-35 and YB-49 bombers of 40 years ago. This was chosen for further development, and contracts were placed not only with the two principals but also with LTV (Vought) for major airframe parts and with General Electric for the engines.

Though the observability — which obviously includes appearance on radar, to human eyes and to sensitive IR (heat) detectors, as well as to noise detectors — naturally grows roughly in proportion to the size and power of an aircraft, the ATB (Advanced Technology Bomber) is expected to be in the same general class of weight and power as a B-1, though its RCS (radar cross-section) may ►

Below: As this book went to press, this was the only official illustration to be released of the ATB. It confirms the over-wing mounting of the four engines, with flat jetpipes.

▶ be only one-hundredth as great. Not much can be done about appearance to eyes, audibility by ears or noise detectors and, especially, the emission of heat from the engines, which varies approximately in relation to total thrust generated. It would have been possible to achieve the desired combat radius with quite a small aircraft, but this would not have been able to carry the specified bombload and other equipment. Accordingly, unofficial reports state that the ATB will be powered by four F101 engines basically similar to those of the B-1B, though of course they will not be augmented and so will be much quieter, smokeless and pump out very much less heat. They will be buried in giant air ducts passing through the centre section of the wing, so that the faces of the compressors cannot be seen from the front, the hot turbines cannot be seen from the rear, the jets are cooled before they leave the aircraft, and no metal hot enough to trigger IR detectors can be seen from astern of the departing aircraft. This is one of the most difficult requirements to meet.

Making the aircraft almost invisible to radars is relatively simple, calling for a blend of carefully arranged smooth shapes and an overall covering of RAM (radar-absorbent material), including dense carbon-packed composite sheets and overall painting with trillions of microscopic ferrite spheres to give a conductive coating. On the Lockheed SR-71 Blackbird an early form of this paint had to be black, but the ATB will probally be grey. Of course, the ATB will emit as little radiation as possible, though it will certainly have comprehensive passive EW installations to warn it of hostile defence systems and assist it in evading detection. Almost nothing will project from the smooth external shape of the wing, and if the crew compartment has any windows these will be completely non-reflective. Surprisingly (because the XB-35 was completely finless) small vertical fins are said to be fitted outboard of the engine bays. Everything else, including all weapons, will be internal.

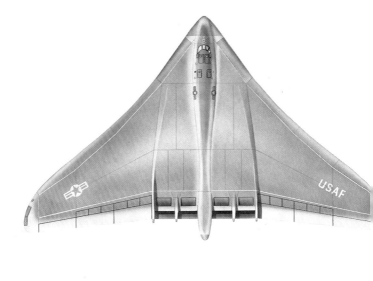

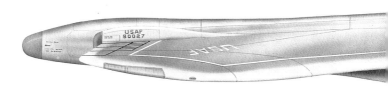

The USAF has a requirement for 132 ATBs, which in service are expected to be designated as the Northrop B-2. Programme price was put at $30 million in 1986 dollars, but in 1986 this was raised to $36 million. A small proof-of-concept ATB is said to have flown in 1982, and a full-scale detailed mock-up was inspected at Pico Rivera in 1985. On the remotest side of the great airfield at Palmdale, where B-1Bs were built, is a large new assembly plant where the ATBs are on the assembly line. The first should have flown before this book appears.

Above: Northrop pioneered "flying wing" aircraft from 1929 onwards. This example, the N-1M, was flown in 1940. It might have had excellent stealth qualities, but nobody thought of such a thing at that time (even in Britain).

Left and below: This artwork was prepared long before there had been an official disclosure of what the ATB actually looked like, and the artist can take credit for not being very wide of the mark. Almost the only major discrepancy is that the engine inlets are actually above the wing (which one might have thought would be more "visible" to radars), though the ducts curve down to flattened jet nozzles which (see previous pages) seem to be below the scalloped trailing edge of the wing.

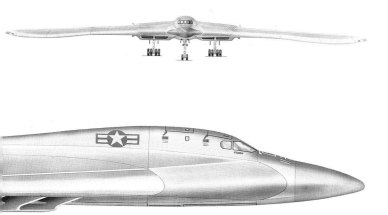

Rockwell B-1A

B-1A

Origin: Rockwell International Corporation (previously North American Aviation), El Segundo, California.

Type: Strategic bomber and missile platform.

Engines: Four General Electric YF101-100 augmented turbofans; thrust stated 'in the 30,000lb/13,608kg class with maximum augmentation', exact figure (under 30,000lb) not being disclosed.

Dimensions: Span (15° sweep) 136ft 8.5in (41.67m), (67.5°) 78ft 2.5in (23.84m); length (with nose boom) 150ft 2.5in (45.78m); height 33ft 7.3in (10.24m); wing area 1,950sq ft (181.2m²).

Weights: Empty (typical) 140,000lb (63,500kg); maximum loaded 389,800lb (176,813kg).

Performance: Maximum speed (clean, high altitude, wings swept 67.5°) 1,320mph (2,124km/h, Mach 2); cruising speed at 500ft (152m) 647mph (1,040km/h, Mach 0.85); combat ceiling, about 62,000ft (18,900m); maximum unrefuelled range (all high altitude) 6,100 miles (5,300nm, 9,817km).

Armament: Three internal fuselage bays in tandem each capable of carrying up to four nuclear bombs, or 25,000lb (11,340kg) of conventional bombs or a rotary launcher for eight AGM-69A SRAM missiles; intended provision for carrying AGM-86 ALCMs, plus four underfuselage hardpoints each capable of carrying 10,000lb (4,536kg) of bombs or two SRAMs; no defensive armament. Note: The four aircraft were completed to different standards, none to what was envisaged as the production configuration.

History: First flight 23 December 1974; first flight of No 4 aircraft, 14 February 1979.

User: Intended for USA (AF).

Deployment: When the famed B-52 was designed it was confidently expected that it would be replaced in SAC service by about 1960. At that time a planned successor did exist in the giant XB-70 Valkyrie, able to fly for long periods at over 2,000mph (Mach 3), but this was cancelled. What followed was a long succession of projects and proposals, one of which, AMSA, actually stood for Advanced Manned Strategic Aircraft but was popularly said to mean America's Most Studied Aircraft! One of the biggest arguments concerned the need for a manned bomber at all, with vast sums being spent on silo-based ICBMs, SLBMs, air-launched cruise missiles and upgrades to the B-52. Other arguments revolved around the kind of bomber that might be needed; the main choices being a traditional machine cruising at high altitude, and able to fly at supersonic speed near the target area, or a very different aircraft designed to rely not on speed but on its ability to evade detection by flying at the lowest possible altitude and carrying the most comprehensive suite of electronic and infrac-infra-red countermeasures.

Eventually, by 1971 the US Air Force had agreed on the design of the North American (Rockwell) B-1 as a traditional supersonic high-altitude bomber, and contracts were placed which, after various changes, called for four flying aircraft, one structural test specimen and 27 engines. The most notable feature of the B-1 was the use of extremely efficient long-span 'swing wings', pivoted well out from the fuselage and able to be moved by irreversible actuators over a range of leading-edge sweep angles from 15° to 67.5°. Powerful slats and slotted flaps could be extended with the wings in their 15° position, giving rapid take-off and relatively slow landing even at high weights. The fixed inboard sections were smoothly blended into the snake-like fuselage, which contained a unique pressurized crew capsule which, in emergency, could be separated from the aircraft, fired clear by groups of rocket motors (which could sense if the capsule was fired with the aircraft inverted, when they would quickly right it) and lowered to the ground to serve as a survival shelter or boat. Propulsion

Above: The No 3 aircraft, 74-01600, was painted in 1980 with this unusual four-colour ''desert camouflage'' scheme.

Below: Another picture of the same aircraft taken just after it was repainted, in February 1980.

▶ was by four completely new turbofan engines in twin groups under the rear of the inboard wing, each engine being fed by a complex variable inlet able to adjust itself to the conflicting demands of slow or Mach-2 flight at different heights. Another unique feature was the SMCS (structural mode control system), comprising devices to sense any unwanted vertical or lateral movements or vibration of the forward fuselage, especially in turbulent conditions, and eliminate it by means of two down-sloping foreplanes near the nose and the lowest of the three sections of the rudder.

The SMCS was added when it was belatedly realised that the B-1 would have to fly its missions at low level, in dense turbulent air. This at a stroke tended to nullify the need for variable engine inlets and the complex and very costly crew capsule, and in October 1974 it was announced that the No 4 aircraft would be completed with conventional ejection seats for the pilot, co-pilot, defensive (avionics) systems operator and offensive (avionics) systems operator. All four aircraft were completed with seats for two further crew, such as instructors, and crew-rest bunks. Fuel was housed in eight integral tanks in the fuselage and wings, and a respectacle for a flight-refuelling boom was provided above the nose in front of the huge bird-proof windshields. The cockpit was of an advanced design, and it was planned to equip it to protect the crew from the blast and radiation of nuclear explosions (during an attack on the SAC base 5 for example), for which reason special arrangements were made to start the engines and get away as quickly as possible.

Flight development of the four aircraft proceeded successfully, and Phase I testing was completed on schedule on 30 September 1976. The Air Force was moving into the production phase when, for various political and budgetary reasons, the incoming Carter administration cancelled almost the entire programme on 30 June 1977. Among other things, it was foolishly said the B-52 (with cruise missiles) could meet SAC's needs virtually indefinitely. Limiting flying continued for a time, and Rockwell continued to improve the design.

Above: Another view of the No 3 aircraft, which also had a huge dorsal spine (it was an electronic waveguide).

Below: The No 2 aircraft had the legend "B-1B TEST PROGRAM" painted on its red/white/blue tail. It crashed in August 1984.

Rockwell B-1B

B-1B

Origin: Rockwell International, North American Aircraft Operations, El Segundo, California.

Type: Multi-role strategic bomber.

Engines: Four 30,750lb (13,948kg) thrust General Electric F101-102 augmented turbofans (thrust given is at sea level with maximum augmentation, afterburning in core and fan flows).

Dimensions: Span (fully spread, to 15°) 136ft 8.5in (41.67m), (fully swept, to 67.5°) 78ft 2.5in (23.84m); length 147ft (44.81m); height 34ft (10.36m); wing area 1,950sq ft (181.2m²).

Weights: Empty 192,000lb (87,091kg); maximum loaded 477,000lb (216,367kg).

Performance: Maximum speed (clean, at 50,000ft/15,240m) 826mph (1,330km/h, Mach 1.25); cruising speed (clean, at 500ft/152m) 700mph (1,127km/h, Mach 0.92); combat ceiling, approximately 60,000ft (18,290m); maximum unrefuelled range (all high altitude) 7,455 miles (6,475nm, 12,000km).

Armament: Three internal weapons bays, comprising a double bay forward of the wing carry-through spar box and a single bay to the rear; the double bay has a movable bulkhead permitting the accommodation of all SAC weapons; total internal capacity for eight AGM-86B or later (Advanced) cruise missiles on rotary launcher, 24 AGM-69A SRAMs on three rotary launchers, 12 B28 or 24 B61 or B83 nuclear bombs, or 84 GP 500lb bombs or 24 GP 2,000lb bombs; alternatively, auxiliary fuel tanks can be installed; eight external stations in two rows beneath the sides of the fuselage for an additional 14 AGM-86B ALCMs or AGM-69A SRAMs, or eight B28s, 14 B43/B61/B83, or 14 2,000lb bombs or 44 500lb bombs; no defensive armament other than electronics.

History: First flight (first production B-1B) 18 October 1984, five months ahead of schedule; first delivery to SAC unit, 7 July 1985; first combat-ready wing, 1986; final delivery (No 100) 1988.

User: USA (AF).

Deployment: In 1977-81 Rockwell and their many contractors worked with the USAF to refine and improve the B-1, and eventually in 1981 defined the B-1B as a proposed production aircraft, the four existing prototypes then being redesignated as B-1As. President Reagan accepted the Air Force's arguments, and on 20 January 1982 Rockwell signed two giant contracts for completion of the design, flight testing of the Nos 2 and 4 B-1As to assist the B-1B, and preparation for B-1B production including delivery of the first aircraft. By 1986 contracts had been placed for all 100 production aircraft, by which time the first 15 were nearing operational capability with the first user unit, the 96th Bomb Wing (BW) at Dyess AFB, Texas.

Above: The No 10 B-1B underwent severe environmental testing in the USAF's McKinley Climatic Laboratory in June 1986.

Below: The No 1 B-1B seen on its third flight in November 1984. Visible wingtip vortices are extremely common.

Compared with the B-1A the B-1B looks very similar, except for its subtly blended grey and dark green camouflage. In fact the two aircraft are very different, and the B-1B has vastly greater capability. One of the greatest differences is that the production bomber is designed specifically for attack at low level, making no concessions to supersonic speeds (though at high altitude fairly high speeds can be attained). A second crucial difference is the greatly increased internal fuel capacity, reflected in the maximum weight. A third is that the B-1B has been designed in the full knowledge of the need for stealth technology, and of the crucial reliance of any modern bomber on its defensive avionics systems. The latter exceed by a wide margin anything previously installed in any aircraft.

Aerodynamically, the chief new features of the B-1B are simplified overwing fairings and totally redesigned engine inlets, with no variable geometry (apart from small hinged lips on each side) but with a sloping vertical splitter between the inlets of each nacelle and with carefully arranged internal baffles to prevent

Right: At least the first five aircraft had white guide lines painted around the inflight-refuelling receptacle. Subsequently low-visibility lines were substituted.

Below: This shows the standard black guide pattern used to assist air refuelling at night.

► the faces of the engine compressors from being visible externally, thus greatly reducing the RCs (radar cross-section) of the aircraft. It has been claimed that, while the B-1A had a RCS one-tenth that of a B-52, the B-1B has an RCS one-tenth of a B-1A! Part of the improvement has been gained by adding RAM (radar-absorbent material) on the skin of various significant parts of the aircraft, while the new paint scheme is a compromise aimed at making the bomber less visible optically. So far as is known, nothing has been done to im-

Below: The mission profile of the B-1 includes a subsonic cruise at high altitude to conserve fuel.

inimise noise or IR (infra-red) emissions, but extremely comprehensive IRCM flare dispensers are carried, adjacent to high-capacity chaff dispensers in the top of the forward fuselage. Like the No 4 B-1A, the B-1B has conventional ejection seats, in a completely redesigned and upgraded crew compartment. A new feature is the use of protective aluminium shielding to prevent nuclear flash-blindness, with six portholes containing windows of PLZT (polarized lead zirconium titanate) which, sensing brilliant light, in 150 millionths of a second ▶

Below: The boomer's view of a B-1B nosing into the correct position where the boomer can "fire" the extensible boom.

► cut out all but 0.003 per cent of the light entering the cockpit.

At the rear of the cockpit are the stations for the OSO and DSO (offensive and defensive systems officers), the defensive system mainly comprising a vast complex of receivers, processors, transmitters and other devices known as the ALQ-161A, and including 108 major 'black boxes' distributed throughout the aircraft. The purpose of this system is to nullify the effect of the aircraft's own presence, detect and counter each hostile threat and generally prevent any enemy anti-aircraft weapon from locking-on to the bom er. Of course, such a system has to be continually updated, to counter each new potentially hostile defence system.

The 96th BW at Dyess is equipped with 29 aircraft, being at full strength in 1987. Next came the 28th BW at Ellsworth (35 aircraft), followed by the 319th BW at Grand Forks and the 384th at McConnell, with 17 aircraft each. Aircraft Nos 1 and 9 have been assigned to continued test and development flying. The 100 aircraft are priced at $238 million each in 1986 dollars, and Rockwell would like to build a further 48 each priced at $195 million.

Right: As noted on page 71, the No 10 aircraft underwent climatic testing in 1986. The photo shows a cold soak test.

Below: The first four aircraft (82-001 and 83-0065) not only had the white refuelling markings but also white-outlined cockpit front windows. They were later repainted.

Tupolev Tu-14 Bosun

Tu-14T

Origin: The A.N. Tupolev OKB, Soviet Union.

Type: Naval bomber and torpedo carrier.

Engines: Two 5,952lb (2,700kg) thrust Klimov VK-1 turbojets.

Dimensions: Span 71ft 1.8in (21.686m); length 71ft 2in (21.69m); height 27ft 3in (8.3m); wing area 725sq ft (67.36m²).

Weights: Empty 31,945lb (14,490kg); maximum loaded 55,886lb (25,350kg).

Performance: Maximum speed (with torpedoes) 525mph (845km/h) at medium heights, 497mph (800km/h) at sea level; service ceiling 37,730ft (11,500m); range (typical mission) 1,870 miles (3,010km).

Armament: Internal bay for 6,614lb (3,000kg) of conventional bombs or two 45-36A torpedoes; four NR-23 23mm cannon, two fixed firing ahead and two in manned tail turret.

History: First flight (Tu-89 prototype) late 1949; service delivery (designation Tu-14) 1951; withdrawal from front-line duty from 1961.

User: Soviet Union (AV-MF).

Deployment: In the years immediately following World War II, Soviet aircraft designers were enormously assisted by the extraordinary decision of the British government to send to Moscow examples of its latest and most powerful turbojet, the Rolls-Royce Nene, of 5,000lb (2268kg) thrust. This was used most notably in the MiG-15 fighter and Il-28 tactical bomber, but it was also used in many other aircraft including a succession of bomber prototypes by the Tupolev OKB. These had two engines slung under a mid/high-mounted unswept wing, and some had a third engine in the tail as an alternative to a gun turret. None of the early prototypes led to production, but by 1948 the Nene had been developed into the more powerful VK-1 engine, and this led to a superior prototype designated Tu-89. In June 1949 the design was accepted for service with the AV-MF as the standard shore-based bomber and torpedo carrier. A series of 500 was ordered, though in the event (possibly because of the higher priority of the Tu-16 'Badger' programme) manufacture was cut short after only about 150 had been delivered. Despite this, the Tu-14 entered combat service and received the NATO reporting name of 'Bosun'.

Below: This Tupolev Tu-81 was an interim prototype differing only in details from the production Tu-14. Previous aircraft in this series had three engines and no tail turret.

► A conventional stressed-skin machine, the Tu-14 was a very clean aircraft handicapped only by the weight of its tail turret, with a pressurized compartment for the gunner. The main crew compartment seated the navigator/bombardier in the glazed nose and the pilot further aft under a glazed canopy, both with ejection seats. Complete night and all-weather equipment was installed, including a ventral radar ahead of the weapon bay. Though marginally underpowered, the Tu-14 was manoeuvrable and reliable, and it proved popular in service. There was also a Tu-14R reconnaissance version, though this is believed not to have been built in quantity.

Right: The standard torpedo bomber was the Tu-14T, and it was roughly contemporary with the I1-28. Rather strangely, at this time the RAF ceased to operate aircraft carrying large anti-ship torpedoes, and has had none since.

Below: Another view of the Tu-14T (it may be the first production aircraft). The front guns are low on each side.

Tupolev Tu-16 Badger

Tu-16 Badger-A, H-6

Origin: The A.N. Tupolev OKB, Soviet Uniion, and Xian Aircraft Company, PRC.

Type: Designed as strategic bomber, today multi-role.

Engines: Two 20,950lb (9,500kg) thrust Mikulin RD-3M turbojets.

Dimensions: Span (without FR attachment) 108ft 0.4in (32.93m), (with FR) 109 ft 11in (33.5m); length (A) 114 ft 2in (34.8m), (D) 120ft 9in (36.8m); height 35ft 5in (10.8m); wing area (no FR) 1,772sq ft (164.65m²), (with FR) 1,819 sq ft 6169.0m²).

Weights: Empty (A) 81,570lb (37,000kg), (typical current version) 92,590lb (42,000kg); maximum loaded (A) 158,730lb (72,000kg), (all known current versions) 169,755lb (77,000kg).

Performance: Maximum speed (typical of current versions, medium altitudes, no external stores) 587mph (945km/h); long-range cruising speed 485mph (780km/h); service ceiling (typical) 42,650ft (13,000m); range (with maximum fuel, all high altitude) 3,980 miles (6,400km), (with maximum bomb/missile load) about 2,980 miles (4,800km).

Armament: Original 'Badger-A' had internal bay for at least two nuclear bombs or up to 19,180lb (9,000kg) of conventional bombs, and seven NR-23 cannon of 23mm calibre, six in three twin turrets and one fixed to fire ahead.

History: First flight (Tu-88·prototype) 1952; front-line service from January 1955; first delivery of H-6, believed 1968.

User: Soviet Union (VVS, AV-MF, Aeroflot), Egypt, Indonesia (inactive), Iraq, China.

Deployment: In mission and timing this aircraft was a counterpart of the B-47 and Valiant, but unlike the Western bombers it has remained in full-scale service to this day, and indeed is still in production in China. It has proved to have an excellent structure with a long life, and to be amenable to conversion to fly missions very different from the high-level strategic bombing for which it was designed in 1949-50. A key to its design was the development of a turbojet which, though rather primitive (and based on German wartime technology), was so large that two sufficed as sole propulsion. The engines are installed at the roots of the long-span swept wings, fed by ducts which curve inwards to improve airflow over the inner wing. Between the engine ducts, under the wing centre-section, is the large bomb-bay. The forward fuselage forms a pressurized compartment which, in the original bomber version, has a navigator/bombardier in a glazed nose (with both visual and radar sighting systems), two pilots on the airline-style flight deck and a radio operator/gunner to the rear with a dorsal sighting dome from which he can command the fire of the forward dorsal and rear ventral turrets. In the tail is a second pressurized compartment for a gunner manning the radar-directed tail guns and, usually, at least one observer looking out through side blisters. The bogie main landing gears retract backwards into large streamlined containers projecting aft of the wing.

The Tu-88 received the VVS (air force) designation Tu-16, and it was a success from the start. About 2,000 were built, and these have since been identified in 11 versions, all of which still appear to be in service. The basic bomber, called 'Badger-A' by NATO, sometimes serves as an air-refuelling tanker, either with a looped hose system joining the tanker's and receiver's wingtips or with a hose-drum and drogue to refuel Tu-22 'Blinders'. The B model carried a turbojet-powered 'Kennel' cruise missile under each wing, but today serves as a conventional bomber. The C version has a giant nose radar and carries a large 'Kipper' supersonic cruise missile recessed under the bomb bay; it has an anti-ship role with the AV-MF. The D model carries a heavy load of electronics instead of weapons and serves in the maritime electronic reconnaissance role. 'Badger-E' has the glazed nose but carries cameras and radars, and 'Badger-F'

Above: The US Navy caption to this splendid picture describes the "bogey" as a "Badger-H", but the rear teardrop radome and blade antennas cannot be seen clearly from this angle.

Below: A "Badger-C Mod", configured for "AS-2 Kipper" but modified to carry a supersonic "AS-6 Kingfish" under each wing.

➤ is similar but adds pylon-mounted electronic-intelligence pods under the wings. The G model is a B converted to launch 'Kelt' rocket cruise missiles under the wings, whilst retaining the bomb-bay. G-Modified has wing pylons for the super-accurate 'Kingfish' supersonic missiles, with a large belly radome. 'Badger-H is an ECM aircraft, with special electronics and 20,000lb (9072kg) of chaff to blind enemy radars. The J variant is a more sophisticated ECM platform, with powerful jammers transmitting from a 'canoe' radome under the fuselage and large plate antennas projecting from each wingtip. 'Badger-K' is an electronic-reconnaissance version, with numerous special avionics devices (mainly receivers and analysers) with the underside of the fuselage dotted with pods and blisters. A photograph has also appeared of an AV-MF version painted white (most 'Badgers' are unpainted) and with a nose pimple looking like the TFR of the Vulcan.

A 1987 estimate of Soviet strength is: VVS, 287 strategic bomber versions, 20 tankers, 15 reconnaissance and 90-110 ECM; AV-MF, 240 attack versions, 75 tankers and about 80 reconnaissance and ECM. Indonesia's Tu-16s are stored, Egypt's have been refurbished with Chinese help, and Iraq has used a small number of Soviet-supplied G versions.

In 1958 the People's Republic of China obtained a licence to build the basic bomber version, but work was halted by the severing of relations with the Soviet Union in 1960. Later the Chinese began work again, and since about 1968 have slowly managed not only to build at least 120, but have developed the Soviet bomber into Chinese versions. The work is centred at Xian, and the Chinese designation is H-6, current production being of the H-6D with a large chin radar of vertical-drum type and wing pylons for two C601 anti-ship cruise missiles with a 62-mile (100km) range. All H-6s so far seen have been white all over.

Above: A beautiful close-up of a "Badger-F", with electronic warfare pods on deep underwing pylons.

Below: Taken in about 1970, this photograph shows a "Badger-D" maritime electronic reconnaissance aircraft, with wide "Puff Ball" nose radar and four blisters along the underside.

Tupolev Tu-22 Blinder

Tu-22A, B, C, D

Origin: The A.N. Tupolev OKB, Soviet Union.
Type: Designed as a medium bomber, modified for reconnaissance and training.
Engines: Two 30,865lb (14,000kg) thrust Koliesov VD-7 turbojets (thrust given is at sea level with maximum afterburner).
Dimensions: Span (estimate) 82ft (25m); length 132ft 11.5in (40.53m); height 35ft (10.67m); wing area 1,650sq ft (155m²).
Weights: Empty (estimated) 90,700lb (40,000kg); maximum loaded 185,000lb (84,000kg).
Performance: Maximum speed 920mph (Mach 1.4, 1,480km/h) at 40,000ft, 550mph (890km/) at sea level; cruising speed (high altitude) 560mph (900km/h); combat ceiling (dry) 45,000ft (13,700m), (afterburner) 60,000ft (18,300m); combat radius (all high altitude, including 249-mile/400km supersonic dash) 1,920 miles (3,100km); ferry range (no dash) 4,040 miles (5,400km).
Armament: (A) Internal bomb-bay two nuclear weapons or 17,600lb (8,000kg) of conventional bombs, and defensive armament of single NR-23 23mm gun in radar-directed remote-controlled tail turret; (B) one 'AS-4 Kitchen' supersonic cruise missile recessed under fuselage, with same tail armament; (C) tail gun only; (D) usually none.
History: First flight (Tu-105 prototype) 1959; service entry believed 1963.
Users: Soviet Union (VVS, AV-MF), Iraq, Libya.

Deployment: The Tupolev OKB (experimental aircraft bureau) began working on supersonic bombers in 1950, and one of the projects became funded as the Tu-98 and flew in 1955. This contained a crew of three, the fuel, bombload, twin afterburning engines and four-wheel bogie landing gears in the finely streamlined fuselage, the engines being fed by huge ducts from inlets near the cockpit. This remained a prototype, but the availability of much larger after-

burning turbojets led to the design of a new bomber prototype, the Tu-105, of more than double the gross weight. This differed in having a huge circular-section fuselage almost entirely filled with fuel, the wing being mounted almost in the low position (leaving room for a short bomb-bay aft of the rear spar) and with the two engines in very efficient pods on each side of the vertical tail. For take-off, the engine duct inlets could be translated forwards to admit extra air round the gaps. The bogie main gears were arranged to retract into typical Tupolev fairings aft of the slim wing, which was swept at the sharp angle of 45° outboard and 50° inboard. The needle-like nose housed a mapping/bombing radar, and immediately to the rear was the pressurized compartment for the navigator/bombardier, with a downward-ejection seat and large windows. Further back sits the pilot, in an upward-ejection seat on the cen-

Above: This Tu-22 was intercepted by F-4Ns of VF-51, from USS *Roosevelt,* as it was being delivered to the Libyan AF.

Below: A "Blinder-D" trainer, seen from under the wing of another. Its three crew doors are hanging open, and the engine inlet cowls are translated forwards (as at take-off).

▶ treline, and the systems officer who also manages the rear gun.

For some reason, the Western official estimate of the range of this extremely large and powerful aircraft — which, despite having only two engines, was heavier and more powerful than the American B-58 Hustler — was only 1,400 miles. Had this been true it would not have been worth building the type in quantity, but in fact the aircraft was designed to fly useful missions and so it did go into production, receiving the VVS designation of Tu-22 and the NATO name of 'Beauty', later changed to 'Blinder'. Tea examples took part in the 1961 Aviation Day airshow, nine being 'Blinder-A' bombers and the tenth a 'Blinder-B'. The latter had a recessed missile and wider nose radome. Features of all production aircraft were an FR nose probe (removable) with internal plumbing, very comprehensive navigation and defensive avionics, and compartments in the rear of the landing-gear fairings for strike cameras and dispensers for chaff, flares and jammers. Seven of the original Blinder-B version were supplied to Libya, one seeing action against Tanzania (on behalf of Uganda). Nine supplied to Iraq have been used against the Kurds and, more recently, Iran. About 135 A and B versions remain operational with VVS Air Armies, plus about 35 with the AV-MF.

In 1965 a dedicated multi-sensor reconnaissance version was identified, and dubbed 'Blinder-C'. This has extensive Elint installations, which vary from aircraft to aircraft, as well as the same six-camera pallet as used by 'Bear-E'. About 60 of this version were built, most remaining in service (including one regiment in Estonia and another in the southern Ukraine). Last of the well-

known variants, 'Blinder-D' is a dual-pilot training version, with most combat equipment removed and with the instructor in a separate pressurized cockpit above and behind the original (pupil) pilot, the raised cockpit reducing dash speed.

Though the Tu-22 family has done everything asked of it, these aircraft have naturally proved expensive to operate, need long and strong runway and have proved difficult to handle following engine-failure (though at light weights a single engine is more than adequate). The combat radius has been adequate for a wide range of missions, though the cheaper Tu-16 family of aircraft have proved much more versatile and useful, and their lack of supersonic dash performance has been no drawback. In wartime, no Tu-22 would attempt to make a high-altitude dash in defended territory under hostile radar surveillance, though the range of the 'Kitchen' cruise missile — 186 miles/300km at low altitude, and considerably more than double this at high altitude — makes a big difference to the Tu-22 B-version's chances of survival, especially in its main role as an anti-warship aircraft.

The Tu-22 was later developed with pivoting 'swing wings', giving much better airfield performance and much greater range and payload capability. The eventual result was the Tu-22M and Tu-26 'Backfire' family.

Below: An unusual view of a "Blinder-A" reconnaissance bomber, showing the Area Rule "Coke bottle" waisting of the huge fuselage above the wing, to reduce supersonic drag.

Tupolev (Tu-26?) Backfire

Tu-22M, Tu-26

Origin: The A.N. Tupolev OKB, Soviet Union.
Type: Multi-role bomber, missile carrier and reconnaissance aircraft.
Engines: Two large augmented turbofan engines; it is generally assumed that these are uprated (perhaps 48,500lb/22,000kg) derivatives of the Kuznetsov NK-144 which powered the Tu-144 supersonic transports.
Dimensions: Span (estimate, with wings swept 18°) 115ft (35m), (55°) 92ft (28m), (65°) 78ft 9in 624m); length (ignoring probe) 140ft (42.5m); height 34ft 6in (10.5m); wing area 1,830sq ft (170m²).
Weights: Empty (estimated) 120,000lb (54,400kg); maximum loaded 286,600lb (130,000kg).
Performance: Maximum speed (clean), (Mach 1.91, 2,036km/h at 36,000ft (11,000m), 680mph (Mach 0.9, 1,100km/h) at sea level; normal cruising speed (medium altitudes) 560mph (900km/h); combat ceiling (dry) 54,100ft (16,500m), (maximum afterburner) 62,300ft (19,000m); combat radius (all high-altitude, DoD estimate) 3,420 miles (5,500km); maximum range 7,500 miles (12,000km).
Armament: Internal bay for unknown number (probably four to six) of nuclear weapons or up to 12,345lb (5,600kg) of conventional bombs, plus 12 or 18 bombs carried on external racks under the sides of the centre fuselage, or alternatively one 'AS-4 Kitchen' supersonic cruise missile recessed under centre fuselage or two Kitchen missiles carried on pylons under the fixed inboard wings; defensive armament of two NR-23 23mm guns in radar-directed remote-controlled tail turret.
History: First flight (Tu-22M) 1969, (Tu-26) believed 1972.
Users: Soviet Union (VVS, AV-MF).

Deployment: In 1969 American satellites photographed the prototype of a large new bomber with variable-geometry 'swing wings' at the vast new factory at Kazan, Tatar ASSR. Careful study showed this to be based on the Tu-22, and it was later learned that it was the first of at least 12 Tu-22Ms which almost certainly were rebuilds of existing Tu-22s. NATO allocated the name ►

Above: This may be the 43rd production aircraft. Later the ''Box Tail'' tail radome was made blunt.

Below: Dubbed ''Backfire-C'', this latest version has ''MiG-25'' type inlets, and may have more powerful engines.

► 'Backfire'. Compared with the original Tu-22 the 'M' version took off and landed in less than half the distance and, because of greater subsonic cruise efficiency with the wings unswept, could fly much further, as well as having the ability to carry much heavier loads. Nevertheless, it was obviously not an optimised aircraft, and though this original 'Backfire-A' did go into limited service, it was not built in quantity (believed 12).

Andrei N Tupolev, the dean of Soviet designers, died in 1972 at the very time that his growing OKB had perfected the Tu-26, or 'Backfire-B'. Though many similarities to the Tu-22 remain, this is in effect a completely new aircraft, with almost doubled capability. The main change is that new and much more powerful engines are installed, with far better fuel efficiency, fed by huge ducts from inlets far ahead of the wings on the sides of the forward fuselage. The latter has been redesigned, the entire needle nose being a radome, the glazed navigator/bombardier compartment being eliminated and a crew of four being accommodated in forward-facing upward-ejection seats arranged two-by-two. The bogie main landing gears retract inwards into the underside of the fuselage. The slab-type horizontal tails were redesigned, and the aerodynamics of the fixed and moving wings refined. The whole structure was restressed to operate at enormously increased weights, as a result of a great increased in internal fuel capacity.

During the original SALT II treaty talks, aimed at limiting strategic (especially nuclear) arms, the Soviet Union emphasized that these aircraft are not intended primarily for strategic attacks on North America (though with one flight refuelling a round trip to the USA is no problem), and accordingly removed their FR probes. These, however, could have been restored in a matter of minutes. Their primary purposes are anti-ship attack in oceanic areas, nuclear or conventional attack on land targets, cruise missile launch against high-value targets, and (it is alleged, though this version has not been seen) reconnaissance. A particular attribute of the Tu-26 is its excellent low-level performance,

which can be sustained at Mach 0.9 for over 1000 miles with no particular crew discomfort. On the other hand, it does not have the specialized low-level ride control of the Rockwell B-1B, nor that aircraft's attention to at least some aspects of stealth design. Like all Soviet combat aircraft, these very large aircraft are richly endowed with defensive electronics, though as these were all designed into the aircraft most of the 30 or more antennas cannot be seen except from very close range. Receivers and jammers cover a considerable proportion of the exterior skin, but, as in the B-1B, they are far from evident. Most Backfires encountered by NATO fighers have been assigned to AV-MF units, and like many of this service's aircraft are painted bluish-grey above, with almost white-grey undersides.

In 1980 a second production version was reported, called 'Backfire-C' by NATO. The main distinguishing feature of this version is that it has wide wedge-type engine inlets, resembling those of the MiG-25 "Foxbat". They can certainly handle a greater airflow, but the engine nozzles appear to be the same size as before, so the reason for the change is puzzling. This version also has a longer, upturned conical nose radome carrying a small pod on its tip which is thought to house avionics rather than be an FR proble.

Deliveries of the Tu-26 began in the mid-1970s. Since then output has been steady at the 30 per year level allowed by the (unratified) SALT II agreement. In late 1987 the number in service was about 300, 200 of them opposing NATO in the West and the remainder in the Soviet Far East. They operate mainly in oceanic areas, co-operating closely with Soviet surface warships and submarines in ways that are of concern to NATO and to Japan, and which have not been practised by forces of the latter nations.

Below: This "Backfire-B" had its wings fully swept, and under the inlet ducts can be seen the detachable racks on which 18 bombs or other stores can be carried.

Tupolev Tu-95/142 Bear

Bear-A

Origin: The A.N. Tupolev OKB, Soviet Union.

Type: Designed as strategic bomber, today multi-role.

Engines: Four 14,795ehp Kuznetsov NK-12MV turboprops.

Dimensions: Span 167ft 6in (51.05m); length (early versions, ignoring FR probe and tailplane pods, if present) 155ft 10in (47.5m), (F) 171ft 6in (52.27m), (H) 164ft 6in (50.14m); height 39ft 9in (12.12m); wing area 3,342sq ft (310.5m²).

Weights: Empty (A, as built) 165,400lb (75,000kg), (F) 178,600lb (81,000kg); maximum loaded (A) 374,800lb (170,000kg), (F) 414,500lb (188,000kg), (H) 418,870lb (190,000kg).

Performance: Maximum speed (typical) 575mph (925km/h) at 25,000ft (7,620m); maximum speed at 41,000ft (12,500m) 518mph (833km(h); high-speed cruise 435mph (700km/h); service ceiling (typical) 44,300ft (13,500m); combat radius in typical ASW/recon/EW mission 5,158 miles (8,285km).

Armament: (A, as built) internal bay for up to four thermonuclear bombs or for convention bombs up to 44,100lb (20,000kg), with defensive armament of six NR-23 23mm cannon in manned tail turret and dorsal and ventral remote-controlled barbettes.

History: First flight about September 1954; service entry late 1956; production of 'Bear-H' continuing in 1987.

User: Soviet Union (VVS and AV-MF), India (reconnaissance/Elint).

Deployment: When this enormous intercontinental bomber became known to the Americans in 1955 it triggered off a massive reaction which, over a period of five years, cost many billions of dollars. This was despite the fact that the Defense Department's estimates of its performance were staggeringly mistaken; in fact, the estimate for this bomber's range was not very different from its true combat radius! What everyone found puzzling was that it had a fully swept wing and tail, yet was driven by propellers. Today our understanding of big ducted fans and propfans is much better, but in 1955 nobody could understand how a propeller aircraft could possibly need sweepback.

The heritage of the Tu-95 can be traced right back to the American B-29 Superfortress, which by 1950 had been developed into the much bigger and more powerful Tu-85. This was not far short of the B-36 Peacemaker in capability, but by this time the way ahead could be seen to an aircraft of far greater capability. The key lay in an enormous turboprop, being developed mainly by a team of captured Germans. When coupled to contra-rotating propellers with broad but thin blades of 18ft 4in (5.6m) diameter, this promised to combine tremendous take off thrust with the cruising specific fuel consumption of a piston engine and the speed of a jet. Fitting four turbo-props in a giant swept-wing aircraft promised a truly impressive range of capabilities, in many ways transcending those of the B-52. At the same time the existing fuselage, complete with its bomb-bays, pressurized crew compartments and operational equipment, (already produced for the Tu-85) could be used with few changes other than a slight increase in length.

As in the Tu-85, the fuselage has an almost perfectly circular cross-section, though the wing was moved from just below to just above the mid position. The crew, which in the original bomber version numbered eight, were accommodated in three pressurized compartments. The biggest, the forward fuselage, houses pilots side by side on the flight deck, and (in the original bomber) two radar/navigators and a bomb-aimer in the glazed nose. A tunnel connected this to a second compartment aft of the wing for what were originally intended to be two engineer/gunners controlling 10 canon in five turrets, the tail turret also having its own gunner in an isolated compartment. Other features included hydraulically boosted flight controls, bogie main landing gears which folded back into streamlined boxes forming a rearwards extension of the inboard engine nacelles projecting well behind the wing, tandem bomb-bays occupying the whole centre fuselage under the wing, and fuel capacity of 16,053 gallons (82,980 litres) in the fuselage and wing. Subsequently this fuel capacity was greatly increased, the forward dorsal and ventral turrets were eliminated together with the mid-fuselage sighting station, and the tail cabin was enlarged to take a second gunner with large side blisters. Later still, an flight-refuelling probe was added above the nose.

Below: From below the huge "Big Bulge" surveillance radar of the "Bear-D" version can be seen clearly.

Foot of page: A "Bear-H" cruise-missile carrier, intercepted by the USAF 21st TFW north of Alaska on 5 April 1985.

From the start of service in 1956 the new bomber, dubbed 'Bear' by NATO, gave the Soviet Union global power it had never previously dreamed of. Without tanker support it was now possible to fly to almost any place on Earth, and Bears were soon being deployed to friendly overseas bases such as Cuba, Angola, Somalia and Cam Ranh Bay in Vietnam. While Western observers continually underrated the capability of these aircraft, and in the early 1960s observed with surprise that they were still in service (though, it was thought, fast being withdrawn and consigned to second-line duties), in fact these unique machines have never ceased to be developed in new versions, never ceased to serve in front-line roles, never ceased to be built, and, in fact, were stepped up in production from Taganvog in 1984 to meet additional requirements. It seems to be difficult for Pentagon analysts to understand that the Soviets build aircraft which not only meet their requirements, but can be kept in use for anything upwards of 30 years.

What is uncertain is how many 'Bears' have been built new for particular roles and how many have been converted. The original VVS designation was Tu-20, but in recent years this has been dropped in favour of the OKB designations. These are Tu-95 for the original variants and Tu-142 for the latest versions built since 1968. Total production of all variants probably amounts to about 500.

The original 'Bear-A' bomber is still in service. Range with a 25,000lb (11,340kg) bombload is about 9,200 miles (14,800km). NATO names for the main and tail-turret radars are 'Short Horn' and 'Bee Hind' respectively, though since 1981 the entire avionics suite has been upgraded and many new antennas have appeared. 'Bear-B' appeared in 1961 and carries the world's biggest cruise missile, called 'AS-3 Kangaroo' by NATO, guided by 'Crown Drum' chin radar. Some aircraft of this version operate in the Elint role with extra avionics and air-sampling canisters under the wings. 'Bear-C can also carry 'AS-3' though its prime role is Elint, with an avionics blister on both sides of the rear fuselage, and often with the tail turret replaced by a long avionics-filled fairing. Bear-D' serves the AV-MF in a multi-sensor reconnaissance role, with a huge 'Big Bulge' belly radar, tailplane tip pods, 'Mushroom' or Short Horn chin radar, bigger tail radar and many other new devices, but retaining the glazed nose. A major role of this version is over-the-horizon target detection for friendly warships and guidance of their cruise missiles. Some of this model

Below: This Tu-95 "Bear-E" was intercepted by F-4s of VF-161 on 7 May 1971. Note the amazing size difference!

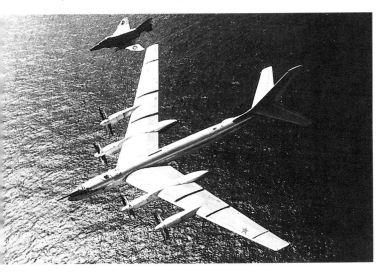

have the long tailcone fairing.

'Bear-E' is a conversion of the original bomber for multi-sensor reconnaissance, with the bomb-bay occupied by large optical cameras and other sensors, and with the left/right Elint installations on the rear fuselage. 'Bear-F' first seen in 1970, is a whole new sub-family (called F Mod I to F Mod IV) of AV-MF Tu-142 aircraft. It has an airframe characterized by complete detail redesign for higher weights, larger tyres requiring bulged nose-gear doors and enlarged main-gear fairings, a redesigned flight deck with a higher roof, deeper windshields and side windows, an extended forward fuselage completely rearranged internally, and many other changes. Unlike the various Elint/recon versions, the fuselage, tailplane tips and other areas are not covered in antennas. Under the fuselage, however, are two radars, one in the chin position and another under where 'Bear-A' has the forward bomb-bay. The role of the F model is ASW (anti-submarine warfare), and it has further enhanced fuel capacity, two stores bays for sonobuoys, torpedoes and nuclear depth charges, no guns except in the tail turret and, in the Mod IV, a MAD (magnetic-anomaly detector) in a long tubular fairing projecting to the rear from the tip of the vertical tail. 'Bear-G' resembles the C version but features six additional or altered avionics items, including pylon-mounted pods under the outer wings, blisters, rails and a pod under the rear fuselage, and a nose thimble (between the FR probe and the main radar) which looks like Vulcan terrain-following radar (also seen on a new AV-MF Tu-16). The weapons comprise two 'AS-4 Kitchen' supersonic rocket cruise missiles, carried on wing pylons, and the long avionics-filled tailcone is fitted.

Most important of the attack versions, in enhanced production since 1984 at a new factory at Kuibyshyev, is another Tu-142 dubbed 'Bear-H'. This has the airframe of the F version apart from retaining the original length of fuselage. It is a dedicated cruise-missile carrier, the primary weapon being the new 'AS-15 Kent' long-range (1,850 miles, 3,000km) cruise missile carried in pairs on inboard wing pylons. The nose has a new deep radar, the fin tip contains new avionics with an antenna extending to the rear, and defensive armament comprises the dorsal and tail turrets only. About 60 were in service in late 1987, and they make dummy attack missions to within 50 miles (80km) of Alaska. Newest of all versions is the 'Bear-J', a naval communications relay platform, which became operational in early 1987.

Below: This "Bear-H" (possibly the aircraft pictured on page 95) was intercepted near Alaska on 3 July 1985.

Tupolev Tu? Blackjack

Designation unknown

Origin: Believed to be the A.N. Tupolev OKB, Soviet Union.
Type: Strategic bomber.
Engines: Four augmented turbofans, each of about 48,500lb (22,000kg) maximum thrust.
Dimensions (estimated): Span (unswept, about 20°) 172ft (52m), (fully swept, about 70°) 101ft (30.75m); length overall 175ft (53.35m); height 45ft (13.75m); wing area 3,500sq ft (325m²).
Weights (estimated): Empty 260,000lb (117,950kg); maximum loaded 590,000lb (267,625kg).
Performance: Maximum speed (clean) about 1,380mph (2,220km/h, Mach 2.09) at high altitude, about 680mph (1,100km/h, Mach 0.9) at sea level; combat ceiling (dry) 55,800ft (17,000m), (maximum afterburner) 65,000ft (20,000m); combat radius (all high altitude, DoD estimate) 4,535 miles (7,300km).
Armament: This aircraft almost certainly has large internal bays for all kinds of thermonuclear and conventional bombs and other air-dropped stores to a total of 36,000lb (16,330kg), probably with provision for rotary dispensers for cruise missiles. It has been stated as a fact by the US Department of Defense that its primary weapons will be the 'AS-15 Kent' air-launched cruise missile, as carried by 'Bear-H', and the new and little-known BL-10 supersonic cruise missile, both of which are said to have a range (presumably at low altitude) of 1,850 miles (3,000km).
History: First flight, probably 1981; production started early 1983; service entry, predicted for 1988.
User: Soviet Union (VVS and possibly AV-MF).

Below: Published in early 1985, this US Defense Department artist's impression purports to show a ''Blackjack'' launching an ''AS-15'' cruise missile, as also carried by ''Bear-H''.

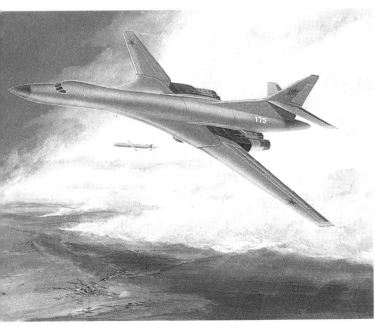

Deployment: That the Soviet Union would require a completely new bomber to replace the long-lived 'Bison' and 'Bear-G' and '-H' in projecting global striking power has long been self-evident, but it was still a considerable shock when what is assumed to have been the first prototype was seen on reconnaissance-satellite imagery on 25 November 1981. The new aircraft was parked on the central test establishment airfield of Ramenskoye, near Moscow, next to two Tu-144 supersonic airliners. This did not necessarily strengthen the belief — which has never been doubted — that the aircraft was designed by the Tupolev OKB, which has doubled in size in the past 10 years and has probably absorbed the staff of the former Myasischyev OKB, but it certainly made it easier to estimate the new bomber's size. The result is awesome, for it is 25 per cent bigger in linear dimensions than the 'Backfire', and thus approximately twice as heavy, and also considerably bigger than the American B-1B. Unlike 'Backfire', whose prime missions are concerned with command of the oceans, the new bomber, given the NATO reporting name of 'Blackjack', is a true intercontinental bomber designed to strike at enemy heartlands in all parts of the globe.

Compared with 'Backfire', which was always to a small degree handicapped by being a direct modification (twice removed) of a quite old existing type, the new bomber is a total 'clean sheet of paper' design. In its general configuration 'Blackjack' follows very closely indeed the Rockwell B-1, though this is simply because it is a sensible arrangement. The crew compartment appears to have the same two-by-two seating for a crew of four (also reported as five), and the engines are possibly of the same type as fitted to 'Backfire' but grouped in pairs under the rear of the fixed inboard wing. Current Western three-view drawings show bogie main landing gears which retract into the engine pods between the ducts, but this is pure speculation because satellites seldom see landing gears. What has often been clearly seen is the beautiful wing, perfectly uncompromised and with much sharper sweep (leading-edge taper) on the inboard ►

Below: Another early Pentagon drawing, illustrating a "Blackjack" at supersonic speed at high altitude with wings at full sweep. It would hardly do this over hostile territory.

▶ section than on 'Backfire', with a straight leading edge from root to tip at the maximum sweep angle of some 70°. It has been repeatedly reported that 'Blackjack' is able to dash at Mach 2, but this is probably of academic interest (except when the bomber needs to cover a lot of territory devoid of hostile defences, where it can fly at high altitude).

It would be common sense to assume that 'Blackjack, like all other modern attack aircraft, would penetrate defended territory at the lowest safe altitude, and thus at about Mach 0.9. The wings would be at maximum sweep not so much for supersonic performance as for minimum gust response, giving the aircraft the smoothest possible ride, assisting the crew to work at maximum efficiency and reduing fatigue damage to the structure. There is not the slightest doubt that this aircraft has been designed to have the best possible stealth features, as well as a tremendously comprehensive EW suite of receivers, jammers, IRCM and other countermeasures, though of course no details are yet known in the West. The 1987 edition of the US Defense Department's annual survey of *Soviet Military Power* contains a drawing showing a 'Blackjack' releasing an AS-15 Kent long-range cruise missile from under the fuselage (probably from an internal rotary launcher). External carriage of bombs and missiles is probably provided for, though this would increase the bomber's RCS (radar cross-section) and reduce flight performance.

In 1986 five prototypes of this enormous aircraft were known to be in flight test. The aforementioned DoD survey stated that the type could enter operational service 'as early as 1988'. It is expected that a production run of at least 100 will be delivered from the gigantic manufacturing complex at Kazan, which, although production of 'Backfire' is probably coming to an end in 1987, has recently had an enormous new assembly hall added. This production complex is as large as all the US military-aircraft assembly halls combined.

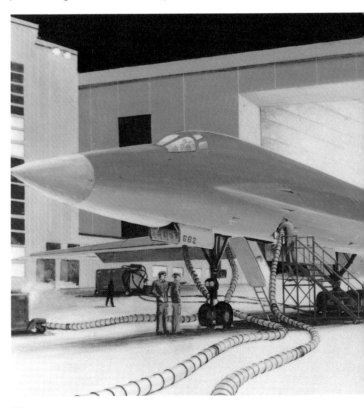

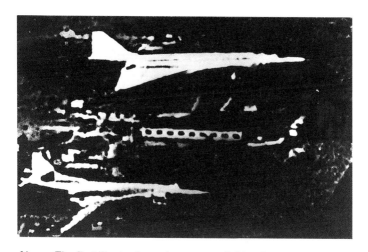

Above: The first illustration to become available of this huge bomber was this satellite image taken of Ramenskoye test airfield on 25 November 1981, showing the prototype.

Below: One of the latest artist's impressions was this Defense Department drawing of 1987, showing "Blackjack" bombers coming off the assembly line at Kazan.

Deployment

One of the biggest revolutions in the technology of the bomber has been in its method of employment. Through World War II, while some bombers attacked at low level — to achieve surprise and high delivery accuracy — most sought to gain as much altitude as possible in order to get above most of the flak and render more difficult the aiming problems of the heavier guns. Reduced bombing accuracy was accepted as an inevitable penalty of this technique. Through the 1950s large bombers continued the same technique, striving for ever-greater over-target height in order to try to escape interception by SAMs (surface-to-air missiles), even though an amateur could see that in due course this philosophy was bound to fail. A few efforts were made to build low-level bombers, but none progressed beyond the prototype stage. As late as 1974, the prototype Rockwell B-1 bomber took to the air as the first of a planned production run of strategic aircraft intended to penetrate hostile airspace at Mach 2 at 50,000ft (15,240m). In view of the demonstrated effectiveness of SAM systems at heights up to (in the case of the Nike Hercules) 130,000ft (40,000m) almost 20 years previously, this appeared foolhardy if not suicidal.

Farsighted navy

While air forces clung tenaciously to high altitudes, naval experts allowed their minds to assimilate the facts. Britain's Royal Navy deserves great credit for seeing what today appears obvious, but which in 1951 was apparently overlooked by everyone else. As radio waves travel — for all practical purposes — in straight lines, the best way to make yourself visible to enemy radars is to fly high. The best way to avoid being seen, on the other hand, is to fly as low as possible, coming in at full throttle beneath the volume of sky swept by the enemy radar(s). In May 1952 specification B.148T and aircraft requirement N.A.39 were issued, calling for

a carrier-based bomber able to perform both these roles. It was a landmark in the design of all bomber and attack aircraft, and it led to the Buccaneer which is still doing an important multi-role attack job today. In 1956, the US Navy followed suit, issuing a requirement for an all-weather low-level bomber which led to the A-6 Intruder, still in full production. These are classed as attack aircraft rather than as bombers, but they exerted a profound influence on the design of large bombers. As the lesson gradually sank in, the B-1 was redesigned to penetrate hostile airspace at subsonic speed at the lowest possible level, even though this meant greatly strengthening the airframe and reducing the aircraft's top speed.

Stand-off weapons

A further change to the method of employment was brought about by the increasing introduction of air-dropped weapons fitted with wings and/or propulsion. This not only greatly increased aiming accuracy but it also enabled the bomber to 'stand off' at a distance from its targets. At first the stand-off distance was a mile or two, but it grew until today it can nudge

2,000 miles (3220km). ASMs (air-to-surface missiles) became smaller, so bombers could carry more of them, and today a proportion can be assigned to so-called 'defence suppression' duty, being aimed at major radars, SAM sites and air-defence headquarters that could pose a threat to the oncoming bomber.

Yet another factor which has a major effect on the radius of action of modern bombes is inflight refuelling. Though pioneered by Britain, it was the USAF which first built up the necessarily large force of tankers, and today SAC (Strategic Air Command) has available some 580 KC-135s and over 40 big KC-10s.

Though a tanker version of the I1-76, dubbed 'Midas' by NATO, is said to exist, the Soviet bomber force has never been supported by a major force of purpose-built tankers. The retaking by Britain of the Falklands would have been impossible without large-scale use of tankers.

Bottom: Flight refuelling is today an essential technique for the fulfilment of combat missions by even the largest aircraft. Here a USAF B-52D takes on fuel from a KC-135A.

Below: Amazingly Britain, which pioneered flight refuelling, built this and many other Valiants with no provision for it but had to add it later. (The Valiant was later a tanker).

Avionics

From World War II onwards it was taken for granted that all bombers would be equipped with radar, which initially was used only in the ground-mapping (or PPI, plan-position indication) mode to give a black/white picture of the terrain and water areas beneath. In almost all bombers, the radar was linked with the optical bomb-aiming system and the aircraft flight-control system, so that reasonably accurate bombing could be made at night or in bad weather. In addition, the expected navigation, communications and bad-weather landing aids would be carried. There was much less uniformity in the matter of ECM (electronic counter-measures) intended to interfere with the enemy's radar surveillance and weapon-direction systems. These had reached a high pitch in World War II, especially with RAF Bomber Command, but in the 1950s and 1960s ECM was often omitted, despite the obviously crucial role it would play in any conflict between major powers.

Upgraded avionics

With the sudden descent to low level, the avionic suite had to be rethought. British V-bombers gained a useful aft-facing ECM installation in the tail, having for years naively believed they could get through to their targets using nothing but an aft-facing radar ('Red Garter') and chaff. When the last surviving V-bomber, the Vulcan, at last recognised it would have to fly its combat missions at low level, it was belatedly given a TFR (terrain-following radar) in the nose to enable the pilot to avoid high ground ahead, especially in bad weather or at night. The USAF's B-52 always had far more comprehensive ECM systems, but these had to be upgraded five times, together with the complex radar navigation and bombing systems, which in any case were twice completely redesigned with successive versions. The switch to low-level operations demanded much better all-weather forward view, and the G and H models accordingly sprouted the twin chin bumps

Below and right: The most prominent modification to B-52G and H bombers has been addition of the EVS. The twin sensors in the chin blisters feed pictorial information on the terrain ahead to cockpit screens.

housing the FLIR (forward-looking infra-red) and LLTV (low-light TV) of the EVS (Electro-optical Viewing System). The EVS presents pictorial information on what is ahead of the aircraft on two large screens in front of the two pilots. Today, the B-52 suite has been dramatically further improved by progressive introduction of the OAS (Offensive Avionics System). This includes completely new inertial and doppler navigation systems, terrain correlation and computers and displays to bring about a fantastic improvement in the accuracy with which the B-52 knows its position at the moment of releasing a SRAM (Short-Range Attack Missile)

or ALCM (Air-Launched Cruise Missile).

Knowledge of a bomber's exact position at crucial points in its mission is of paramount importance. Today, the latest US bombers are about to be integrated with the Navstar GPS (Global Positioning System), which could reduce CEP (circular error probability) by a further 87 per cent. With the GPS receiver in use a B-52, a B-1B or ATB (Advanced Technology Bomber) should be able to 'tell' its missiles their position in three-dimensional space at the moment of launch to within 30ft (10m), even after a flight lasting thousands of miles.

Future bombers, all of totally 'stealth' design, will still have to be packed with avionics. The ATB, as described by USAF General McMullen, will have 'an array of sensors to detect EM emissions, a high-resolution radar and IR sensors'. These will be needed not for accurate navigation but to enable the aircraft to do its primary job to seek and find mobile targets, such as rail-mounted ICBMs (Intercontinental Ballistic Missiles). In any conceivable war between the superpowers, great efforts would be made to decoy bombers away from the real mobile targets by enticing them to sophisticated decoys. These decoys would not just look like the real thing, they would have the correct radar and IR spectral responses and make the correct EM emissions. The bomber's avionic sensors have to be sophisticated enough to see through such deception, yet be used in such a fleeting and covert way that they do not compromise the bomber's own stealthy flight. Where possible the mission would be assisted by friendly reconnaissance satellites, but (despite SDI) it is considered problematical that such spacecraft would survive long in a future war.

Flight performance

The greatest advance in aircraft flight performance took place over the approximate time frame of 1945-60. In those 15 years, speeds multiplied by more than five and operating height by more than two, while typical bomber ranges were greatly extended despite the switch to jets (which was originally expected to result in reduced range) and great increases in bombloads. Part of the increase came suddenly, with the switch from piston to jet engines in the immediate aftermath of World War II. A further dramatic advance in speed and height came in the mid-1950s with the introduction of the B-58 Hustler (Mach 2 at over 65,000ft/2440m), and a further leap to a new plateau (Mach 3 at 80,000ft 24,400m) with the B-70 Valkyrie around 1960. What was not expected, however, was that thereafter the trend would be sharply downwards. With the need to penetrate hostile airspace at the lowest

possible altitude it became impossible to fly at high supersonic speeds except over the sea, and even in the latter case the bomber has to be stressed to withstand extremely severe inflight loads caused by the enormous dynamic pressure. (Dynamic pressure, in effect the force exerted by the air on each unit of area of the bomber's skin, is proportional to the square of the speed multiplied by the air density. Previously, the increases in speed had been accompanied by much greater altitudes, resulting in very low air density, but high speed at low level gave rise to very severe stress problems). In addition, high speed at low level would imply an extremely high rate of fuel consumption.

Until the late 1960s, interception by fighters was a very important consideration in the design of a bomber. Even today such interception is important, but it is likely to take place

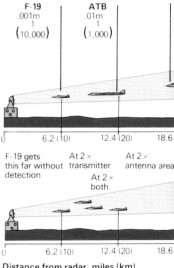

Distance from radar: miles (km)

Above: The top diagram shows in rough outline how close particular USAF aircraft ('F-19' is symbolic of the Lockheed reconnaissance/strike aircraft) can get to a hostile radar before being detected. The diagram immediately above shows what the enemy can do by doubling his radar power, antenna area or both together.

from a much greater distance. Thus, the previous generation of bombers might find themselves in almost a dogfight situation.

Below: The B-52 showed little regard for head-on radar cross-section, but the B-1A bore it in mind and the B-1B engine inlet design was dominated by it.

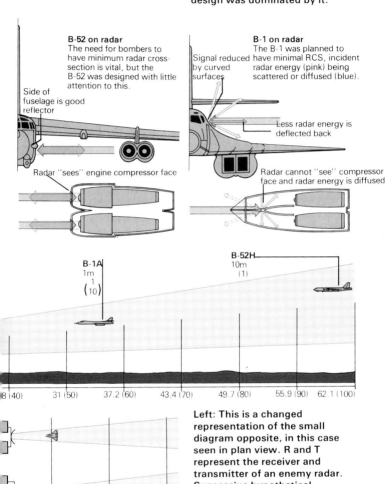

B-52 on radar
The need for bombers to have minimum radar cross-section is vital, but the B-52 was designed with little attention to this.

Side of fuselage is good reflector

Radar "sees" engine compressor face

B-1 on radar
The B-1 was planned to have minimal RCS, incident radar energy (pink) being scattered or diffused (blue).

Signal reduced by curved surfaces

Less radar energy is deflected back

Radar cannot "see" compressor face and radar energy is diffused

B-1A
1m
$\left(\frac{1}{10}\right)$

B-52H
10m
(1)

8 (40)   31 (50)   37.2 (60)   43.4 (70)   49.7 (80)   55.9 (90)   62.1 (100)

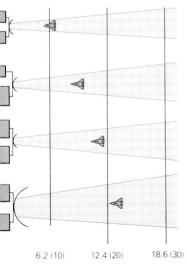

Left: This is a changed representation of the small diagram opposite, in this case seen in plan view. R and T represent the receiver and transmitter of an enemy radar. Successive hypothetical versions of this radar show a 'doubled power' transmitter, a doubled transmitter and receiver, and a doubled output transmitter and receiver in combination with an antenna of doubled area. The scale along the bottom gives an approximate indication of how close a 'stealth' aircraft could approach each radar without being detected. Such considerations are likely to dominate the design of all future bombers.

6.2 (10)   12.4 (20)   18.6 (30)

Interception

Today the bomber's altitude performance is likely to be of no practical interest, while its speed and agility at low level are virtually certain to be inferior to those of intercepting fighters and their AAMs. The most difficult task of the interceptor is to detect the bomber and lock its sensors (radar and/or FLIR) onto it, despite the very close proximity of the Earth's surface immediately beyond it. The interceptor is likely to detect the bomber from a location from several miles to tens of miles astern of i t, and perhaps 10 miles higher — provided it has an effective 'look down, shoot down' radar. The only aspect of the bomber's flight performance that might be important would be its ability, if so designed, to make sudden lateral movements without the need to bank into a conventional turn. The USAF F-16/AFTI (Advanced Fighter Technology Integration), with combined forward oblique canards and a rear rudder, is one of the few aircraft flying today that can do this. Making such a last-moment computerized lateral dodge should enable the bomber to escape beyond the lethal radius of the missile's warhead. Even if it could pull far more g in a turn than the bomber, the missile's much greater speed would make it impossible for it to follow the bomber's sudden dodge. So far as the author knows, no bomber (not even on the drawing boards) has this capability. The required vertical aerodynamic control surfaces could be retractable, and extended only when needed.

Weapons I: Bombs

Apart from a few primitive ASMs steered into their targets by a member of the bomber crew via a radio link, the only weapons carried by bombers at the start of the 1950s were unguided bombs, mines and similar parcels of explosives. Some were designed to skip or ricochet along the surface of the water, for attacking ships or dams, while others had rocket propulsion to help them penetrate the massive roofs of U-boat shelters (which were typically 14 to 20 times thicker than today's hardened aircraft shelters). All were very much hit-or-miss weapons, and

the likelihood of a hit on a target even as large as an aircraft hangar was normally less than 50 per cent at 10,000ft (3km), 15 per cent at 20,000ft and 5 per cent at 30,000ft.

In 1951 the author was told by the AOC of RAF Bomber Command, then Air Chief Marshal Sir Hugh Pughe Lloyd, 'We have simply got to get away from this free-falling bomb business as quickly as possible'. This was an interesting comment, coming as it did at the very time that the Command was about to re-equip with jet bombers carrying nuclear weapons. There were several reasons behind the desire for better aiming accuracy. One was the fact that conventional bombs continued to be important; for example, in attacking a widely dispersed hostile fleet, it would not be altogether desirable to drop a nuclear bomb on every vessel. Though hardly apparent in 1951, there was to develop a new class of superhardened targets, notably ICBM missile silos, where even with nuclear weapons extremely high accuracy was going to be needed to have any significant effect (being fixed, such targets would be attacked chiefly by their own kind, namely ICBMs).

Nuclear weapons

The first nuclear bombs were large (typically 9,000lb/4000kg weight) and rather clumsy, while the first thermonuclear or 'H-bombs' were considerably larger still. The V-bombers and B-52 were all designed to be capable of carrying a single bomb with a length of over 25ft (7.6m) and a diameter exceeding 8ft (2.4m). Gradually, especially in the 1950s, the design of nuclear weapons made such dramatic progress that, while yields (the equivalent masses of TNT high explosive to achieve the same blast effect) multiplied, the volume and weight of the bombs was reduced. Certainly the most important of the early US free-fall bombs was the B28, made in very large

Right: The ultimate bomb trucking system was the B-52D with Big Belly modifications for up to 60,000lb internally and 24 bombs (500 or 750lb) externally.

numbers in tactical as well as strategic versions, with the same nuclear device packaged in sharply different ways depending on the application. The strategic version, which has a 'normal' though parallel-sided bomb shape, with a rear tail, can have a yield of up to 2.8MT (2.8 million metric tonnes of TNT), yet weighs only 5,500lb and is often carried by B-52s in groups of four loaded as one unit.

Below: An unusual view of a Vulcan B.2 of the RAF taken in the 1960s when these aircraft were fully operational with the Blue Steel supersonic stand-off missile. Note the bulged tailcone for Red Steer tail-warning radar, and the ECM flat antenna beneath the two right-hand jetpipes. Later passive warning receiver antennas were added in a fin-top fairing.

In the case of B28, typical of thousands of nuclear bombs of the period 1958-78, the common warhead core has a composition made up of Plutonium-239 and Lithium-6 deuteride, seeded with tritium (the rare isotope of hydrogen of atomic mass 3). The surrounding implosion system comprises a multiple array of shaped charges of Cyclotrol/PBX-9505 high explosive. The most common B28 warhead device has a length of 36in (915mm) and a diameter of 20in (508mm), demonstrating the amazing progress made during the 1950s in reducing the size of even high-yield thermonuclear devices. The basic device could be tuned to give any of five yields: 70 or 350kt (kilotonne), or 1.1, 1.45 or 2.8MT. The original Mod 0 bomb of 1958 weighted 2,540lb (1152kg). The later Mk 4 version was streamlined for external carriage yet weighed only 2,0216lb (919kg), complete with radar fuzing for air- or ground-burst detonation. There are many other variants of the B28, some streamlined and others bluff finned bombs for internal carriage, and several with the option of a parachute

to slow the bomb and give the bomber time to escape its effects. Versions intended for 'laydown' — release in level flight at low altitude — can have a lifting aerofoil parachute which actually makes the bomb climb into the sky while the bomber escapes from the target area at full throttle.

Toss bombing

This form of low-level delivery is an alternative to the LABS (Low-Altitude Bombing System) manoeuvre which is usually practised more by agile fighter and attack aircraft than by large bombers, whose structures are sometimes not stressed for such a punishing manoeuvre. In the LABS delivery the aircraft is brought in at full throttle low over its target and then, either flown by the pilot or under autopilot control linked to the weapon-delivery aiming system, it is pulled up into the first part of a loop. As the bomber reaches the almost vertical attitude the bomb is released. The bomber can then either push over and continue straight ahead or continue the loop until it is inverted and go back the way it came. It has a

minute or more in which to escape, this being the time the bomb takes to rise high in the sky, come virtually to a stop, pitch over and then fall on the target. There are two forms of LABS, the forward delivery in which the bomb is released at a climb angle of some 85° and the over-the-shoulder toss in which the bomber does not release the bomb until it is climbing at 90°, thereafter continuing on round to go back the way it came. It would be rare for a large strategic bomber to overfly an NW (nuclear weapon) target.

Nuclear accident

The B28 was described in some detail as being typical of large numbers of free-fall nuclear bombs. Today there are about 900 B28s of all types still in the USAF inventory, most having been replaced by the smaller and more advanced B83. Today's nuclear weapons have high-explosive implosion systems almost immune to detonation unless deliberately commanded — unlike the B28 which in January 1966 suffered two unwanted implosion explosions in bombs which fell on Spain when a B-52 was destroyed in a mid-air collision with a tanker. The detonations ripped the bombs apart, and released some radioactive material, but, thanks to the exceedingly complex and (believed) foolproof safety/arming systems, did not implode the cores to the critical point at which a thermonuclear explosion could occur. Today it can (it is confidently believed) be guaranteed that no accidental drop of a free-fall nuclear bomb can cause any kind of explosion whatsoever. The same considerations, almost exactly, apply to nuclear mines and depth charges, which are sometimes carried by strategic bombers assigned to sea control and other maritime missions.

Below: An F-111A of the USAF flying from Edwards AFB in October 1976 with a test B77 nuclear bomb. One of literally thousands of nuclear bombs developed during 1958 to 1978, this weapon was cancelled two years later. The bomb's bright colours are for test purposes, operational bombs being grey or silver.

Weapons II: missiles

None of the first generation of jet bombers, such as the Canberra, B-47 Stratojet or Valiant, carried any kind of ASM in combat service (excluding short-range tactical ASMs carried by the Canberra B.6). On the other hand, the next generation, such as the B-52 and Vulcan, and modified Soviet 'Badger' and 'Bear' bombers, all carried missiles notable for their massive size and weight, which reflected the size of their warheads and their large fuel capacity. Today's missiles for similar missions are so small that large numbers can be carried inside a bomber's weapon bays.

Chronologically, the first of the crop of large missiles to enter service (in December 1959) was the North American AGM-28 Hound Dog. Two of these could be carried on large pylons under the inner wings of the B-52G. Though very slim, Hound Dog was nearly 45ft (13.7m) long, and it had a canard delta layout rather like a modern air-combat fighter, though one very prominent feature was the relatively bulky J52 turbojet, of 7,500lb (3,402kg) sea-level thrust, slung under the fuselage at the rear. The J52 engines of the two Hound Dogs were normally started and run up to full thrust to help the heavy bomber take off; then they were shut down until near the point of missile release. Hound Dog weighed 9,600lb (4,350kg) and carried a W28 (one of the B28 family) thermonuclear warhead over a range of up to 600 miles (966km) at a speed of up to Mach 2 (1,320mph/2124km/h). Each Hound Dog was stored attached to its pylon, which contained an astro-tracker able to navigate by the stars, thus continuously updating the missile's position which was fed in from the B-52's inertial system at the moment of launch. The bomber crew could alter the missile's target location or its flight profile (changes of altitude) or route to be followed at any time up to the moment of launch. After 1965 most missiles were of the AGM-28B type, specially modified for low-level operations (which reduced speed and range considerably). Hound Dog was withdrawn from the inventory of USAF Strategic Air Command in 1976.

A planned successor to Hound Dog was GAM-87A Skybolt. This was an impressive ALBM, a kind of delivery system worked on by several US companies in the 1950s and matured in the Douglas Skybolt of 1960. A wingless rocket with eight tail fins, Skybolt was too big for internal carriage so it had a tail fairing which increased its length to 38ft 3in (11.66m), launch weight being 11,300lb (5126kg). Various arrangements on the B-52 and Vulcan were studied for up to six of these virtually unstoppable weapons, which carried a thermonuclear warhead a distance of up to 1,150 miles (1,850km). Planned as a major weapon for both the USAF and RAF, Skybolt was surprisingly terminated by President Kennedy in December 1961, for reasons which appeared to be political rather than technical.

British deterrence

Britain's Blue Steel 'stand-off bomb' was in full engineering development as early as 1954, but it took

so long to mature that not one reached user squadrons until 1962. Ultimately, in 1964, Blue Steel was operational with squadrons flying both the Vulcan B.2 and Victor B.2, each aircraft carrying a single missile recessed under the belly. A massive canard delta like Hound Dog, Blue Steel differed by having liquid rocket propulsion which reduced range to a maximum of 200 miles (322km). It had a short life, being withdrawn from 1973, and various improved versions were cancelled, since when Britain has had no strategic bomber capability.

Above: Fuelling a Blue Steel in special clothing because of the reactivity of the HTP (high-test peroxide) used in the rocket engine.

Below: A class of students at Chanute AFB in 1961 receiving instruction in the maintenance of the Hound Dog cruise missile.

In the Soviet Union a succession of cruise missiles, noted more for their massive size than advanced design, began to be seen by Western observers from the late 1950s. The first was dubbed by NATO 'AS-1 Kennel', and it looked like what it was: a miniature version of an early swept-wing jet by the MiG bureau. Powered by a small turbojet, it weighed about 6,600lb (3,000kg) and had a range of up to 93 miles (150km) against major ship targets, flying part of the way on autopilot and using its own nose radar above the engine air inlet for the final homing on the target. The 'Badger-B1' version of the Tu-16 could carry one of these subsonic missiles under each wing. A later Tu-16, called 'Badger-C' appeared in 1961 with a much larger and faster missile carried under the fuselage. Called 'AS-2 Kipper', this faintly resembled the USAF's Hound Dog in having a powerful turbojet underslung under the rear fuselage, but it appeared to be unlike the US missile in having a radar for homing on moving targets, such as major ships. Roughly 31ft (9.4m) long, Kipper was thought to cruise at Mach 1.2 and have a range of 132 miles (212km).

At the same 1961 air display that revealed AS-2, giant 'Bear' bombers were seen carrying an even larger ASM, which NATO called 'AS-3 Kangaroo. Larger than any other bomber-launched weapon, this mis-

sile again looked very like a jet fighter, having a straight-through fuselage with nose inlet resembling a MiG-21, highly swept wings and tailplane and an almost untapered sweptback vertical tail. Length was about 49ft (15m), long launch weight about 22,000kg (10,000kg), and range about 400 miles (650km) with a nuclear or very large conventional warhead. Again, this was thought to be primarily an anti-ship missile, individually able to cripple the most powerful warship, but the method of guidance over such a long beyond-the-horizon range has never been disclosed.

Soviet proliferation

Yet another disclosure at the 1961 air display was a totally different supersonic missile called 'AS-4 Kitchen', carried recessed under the belly of a special version of the Tu-22 'Blinder'. Unlike its predecessors, this was rocket-propelled and cruised at over Mach 2 for a range of no less than 400 miles (650km) at high altitude, or 185 miles (300km) at very low level. This tailed-delta missile, which is still in wide service on the Tu-16, Tu-22 and Tu-26, is about 37ft (11.3m) long and has a launch weight of more than 13,228lb (6,000kg). Guidance is believed to be inertial, with very accurate radar terminal homing. The version with a large conventional warhead has been used by Tu-22s of the Iraqi air force.

In 1968 a new version of the ubiquitous Tu-16 'Badger' appeared, carrying a rocket missile under each wing which received the NATO name of 'AS-5 Kelt'. It looked like an upgraded 'AS-1', with clear MiG features including the sharply swept wings and tail and very broad swept-back vertical tail. Missiles of this type in Egyptian service have been studied by Western observers, who have noted the great size of the nose radome. Apparently, most of the mission is flown on autopilot, the radar finally being used in an active or (if possible) passive mode, (the latter requiring tuning to emissions from the target). Several Egyptian 'Kelts' were used against Israeli radar stations in 1973. This portly missile weighs 7,716lb (3,500kg) and has a range of 100 miles (161km) at Mach 0.9 at low level, or more than twice this distance at Mach 1.2 at high altitude.

First seen in the early 1970s, 'AS-6 Kingfish' is very similar to 'AS-4' in shape, but is smaller, shorter-ranged and much faster, having a cruising speed of up to Mach 3. It may use the same rocket motor. Guidance is initially inertial, followed by particularly active terminal radar homing. It would be logical for later versions also to incorporate terrain-comparison systems, in which the missile navigates with extreme precision by comparing the varying undulations of the ground below with information stored in its memory. This missile carries a 200KT nuclear warhead or a large HE warhead, and flies 135 miles (220km) at sea level, or about 300 miles /483km) at high altitude.

Below left: 'Backfire-B' seen by J35F Draken of the Swedish air force over the Baltic sea. The bomber is carrying a single cruise missile (called AS-4 Kitchen by NATO) recessed under the fuselage (see picture below). It is also equipped with racks under the outer sides of the fuselage for 12 bombs of 500kg (1,102lb) each.

Below: Western analysts learned a lot from this close-up photograph of an AS-4 Kitchen, which can fly 186 miles (300km) at Mach 4.6. It exists in several versions: anti-ship with HE warhead, nuclear (350 kilotonnes), defence suppression (passive radar homing), and a nuclear version with active terminal radar.

The latest known Soviet missile carried by strategic bombers, 'AS-15 Kent' is a cruise missile of the most modern type, entering service carried by 'Bear-H' in 1984. While attached to the bomber it resembles a torpedo. Upon being released, the wings and tail unfold, the inlet for the air-breathing engine (probably a small turbofan) is hinged open and the guidance system is activated. Measuring about 23ft (7m) in length 'AS-15' is estimated to carry a thermonuclear warhead over ranges up to 1,864 miles (3,000km), using terrain-comparison and inertial guiance for extreme accuracy (terminal error is reported to be well within 150ft/45m). This missile appears to be an exact counterpart of the American Tomahawk and, like the US weapon, there are versions for use from ground vehicles and from submarines.

Chinese puzzle

The People's Republic of China has developed an anti-ship missile which appears to owe much to the Soviet 'AS-5 Kelt' and 'SS-N-2 Styx', the latter being a ship-launched weapon. Carried under the wings of H-6 ('Badger'-type) bombers, this portly rocket weapon is designated C601, but NATO calls it 'CAS-N-1'. It has midcourse inertial guidance and monopulse terminal radar homing, and the Chinese have claimed that it is considerably more advanced in guidance accuracy and resistance to countermeasures than similar Soviet weapons. Despite having an 1,102lb

Below: A 1982 launch by B-52G (over the Pacific near Vandenberg AFB) of an AGM-86B ALCM. Note the low level.

Below right: AN FB-111A of USAF Strategic Air Command releasing AGM-69 SRAM (Short-Range Attack Missile).

(500kg) warhead, C601 is smaller (24ft 3in/7.38m) and lighter (5,380lb, 2440kg) than 'Kelt', and it flies 62 miles (100km) at Mach 0.9 at very low altitude.

America's cruise missile

In 1964 the USAF drafted a requirement for a SRAM, carried in multiples aboard large bombers to help defeat defences. This is still in wide service, but has now been supplemented by a subsonic weapon which, via a shorter AGM-86A version, matured in 1979 as AGM-86B, better known as the ALCM. An extremely neat weapon, AGM-86B has a long but slim body of almost triangular section, housing sufficient fuel for a range at 500mph (805km/h) of 1,550 miles (2,500km). Folded compactly, tandem triplets can be carried on the inner pylons under the wings of a B-52G (later B-52H also), while eight can be loaded onto the internal rotary dispenser. The B-1B carries eight internally and 14 externally. Each missile is programmed to attack a point target via a route which varies in plan and profile to render interception difficult. Upon release the wings, tail and engine inlet unfold, the 600lb (272kg) Williams F107 turbofan is started, and navigation proceeds by inertial means updated and refined by Tercom (terrain comparison) to give great accuracy to the warhead. The latter is usually a W80 nuclear device of 150KT yield. Launch weight is 3,200lb (1,450kg). The USAF received 1,715 of these versatile missiles.

Today, General Dynamics is well advanced in development of the completely new AGM-129 ACM (Advanced Cruise Missile). Work began in 1983 on this weapon, which will, from about 1990, augment and later replace the ALCM. ACM is a true stealth missile, virtually impossible to detect by existing defence systems. The Williams F112 turbofan has a high bypass ratio, resulting a very cool and quiet jet which is difficult to hear or detect by IR sensors. Range will be at least 2,000 miles (3,220km), carrying a W80-1 warhead with a yield of about 200KT. The USAF expects to buy an initial batch of 1,261 ACMs to arm B-52H and B-1B.

France's deterrent

The only other current bomber missile is France's ASMP (Air-Sol Moyenne Portée, air-ground medium-range). Carried by the Mirage IVP supersonic bomber, and also by the small Mirage 2000N, the ASMP is a slim weapon with a length of 17ft 8in (5.38m) and a weight of 1,985lb (900kg). It cruises at Mach 3 on the sustained thrust of an internal ramjet, giving it a range of 62 miles (100km) carrying a high-yield (150kT) nuclear warhead. ASMP is for use mainly against high-value targets, especially those of a mobile nature which could not readily by hit by France's SSBS or MSBS ballistic missiles. At present, however, its guidance system is of the inertial-plus-Tercom type, which makes it suitable only for fixed targets.

Defeating the defences

For over 30 years, bombers have carried various devices other than plain chaff and jammers, or IRCM flares, to help them avoid being shot down over enemy territory. Much more sophisticated was the ADM-20 Quail, developed from 1955 for the B-52 and carried by that aircraft until 1979. Quail was a miniature aeroplane, made mainly of glassfibre and powered by a General Electric J85 turbojet giving the 1,100lb (499kg) vehicle a range of 250 miles (400km) at the same speed as the B-52. With wings and tail folded, up to three could be carried in the weapon bay along with nuclear bombs. The Quails could be released in hostile airspace, each mimicing the B-52 and thus diluting and confusing the defences.

For many years there were plans to replace Quail with a more advanced AGM-86 SCAD (Subsonic Cruise Armed Decoy) missile, but this was never funded. Unlike Quail, SCAD would have carried a nuclear warhead, so none could be ignored by the defences. Instead, the SAC B-52 force was armed with AGM-69A SRAM (Short-Range Attack Missile). Strategic Air Command still has about 1,150 of the 1,500 SRAMs, but their motors and electronics have deteriorated and warhead safety is no longer regarded as equal to the desirable level. After prolonged study of an update programme the decision was taken to buy new missiles. SRAM II is expected to fly at over Mach 3. Launch weight will be similar to that of AGM-69A, which weighs 2,230lb (1,012kg), and range should be a little greater. The warhead will probably be the same W80-1 as fitted to the long-range ACM.

It has been speculated that SRAM II might be used against aerial targets, such as the Il-76 'Mainstay' airborne warning and control aircraft. Such use is entirely feasible, though it would be grossly inefficient. Instead of modifying SRAM II to home on such targets (which would need a different guidance system), it would be better to use a missile with much greater range and a less cataclysmic warhead than the 200kT W80. In due course the B-1B and ATB may well be armed with air-to-air missiles specially intended for knocking out AWACS-type aircraft and possibly even defending interceptors, but neither ACM nor SRAM II seems the best basis for such a missile.

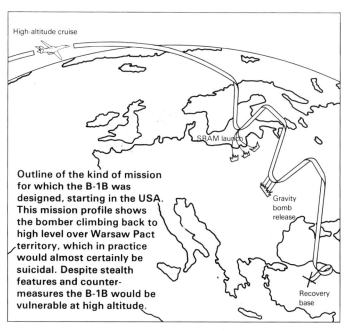

High-altitude cruise

SRAM launch

Gravity bomb release

Recovery base

Outline of the kind of mission for which the B-1B was designed, starting in the USA. This mission profile shows the bomber climbing back to high level over Warsaw Pact territory, which in practice would almost certainly be suicidal. Despite stealth features and countermeasures the B-1B would be vulnerable at high altitude.